PIANO PIECES

NORTH POINT PRESS

Farrar, Straus and Giroux

New York

R u s s e l l   S h e r m a n

PIANO PIECES

North Point Press

A division of Farrar, Straus and Giroux

19 Union Square West, New York 10003

Copyright © 1997 by Russell Sherman
Printed in the United States of America

First published in 1996 by Farrar, Straus and Giroux

First North Point paperback edition, 1997

The Library of Congress has catalogued the hardcover edition as follows:
Sherman, Russell.

Piano pieces / Russell Sherman.

p.   cm.

ISBN 0-374-23206-7

1. Music—Philosophy and aesthetics.   2. Piano music—History and
criticism.   3. Piano—Instruction and study.   4. Music and society.
I. Title.

ML60.S5178   1996

786.2—dc20   95-25707

                                              MN
Grateful acknowledgment is made for permission to reprint the following: Excerpts
from *The Tuning of the World* by R. Murray Schafer with permission of Alfred A.
Knopf/Random House. Copyright © 1977. Excerpts from *The Bow and the Lyre* by
Octavio Paz, translated by Ruth L. C. Simms with permission of the University of
Texas Press. Copyright © 1956 Fondo de Cultura Económica. Renewed 1973 by
Octavio Paz. Excerpts from *Great Composers: Reviews and Bombardments* by Bernard
Shaw with permission of The Society of Authors on behalf of the Bernard Shaw
Estate. Copyright © 1978. Excerpts from *The Music of Liszt* by Humphrey Searle
with permission of Dover Publications, Inc. Copyright © 1966. Excerpts from *The
Theories of Claude Debussy* by Léon Vallas with permission of Dover Publications, Inc.
Copyright © 1967. Excerpts from *Gerard Manley Hopkins: A Selection of His Poems
and Prose,* edited by W. H. Gardner, with permission of Oxford University Press.
Copyright © 1953. Excerpts from *Letters on Cézanne* by Rainer Maria Rilke, translated
by Joel Agee with permission of Fromm International. Copyright © 1985. Excerpts
from *Mozart's Letters,* edited by Eric Blom, translated by Emily Anderson, with permission of Macmillan UK. Copyright © 1956.

For my wife, Wha Kyung Byun

CONTENTS

ò

PREFACE

The prospect of summing up one's thoughts, of providing an account of the accumulated wisdoms, insights, and anecdotes of one's life experience, has always seemed to me equally attractive and vain. Fortunately, since I am rather lazy in most respects, the idea for attempting such a project never burdened me greatly. And even if I had never accomplished the reluctant deed, I would always feel much worse for not committing to fingers and memory the forty-eight Preludes and Fugues of Bach, the pianist's Old Testament according to Busoni.

But here is the outcome, nevertheless, and in fact approached with a certain passion. For it turns out that there are many things worth saying about piano playing and related topics, things which others might well say better, but yet deserve to be whispered or shouted, however crudely, according to which gospel you believe. And God knows, I have beliefs, for I react madly or badly to the tides of the day, while those of my past bring back many fond and urgent memories.

Enclosed, then, is the diary of an old and unregenerate crust. And yet, this curmudgeon still has the most youthful and passionate relations with the music he plays and studies. It is patently clear that I am the youngest pupil in my studio. The others, though superb, are occasionally a bit tired and enervated. It must have something to do with the times, their insidious assault on our brains and senses, leaving us rather numb and glum.

And so I offer these jottings as a testimony to the powers and seductions of music, trying to scrape off those barnacles of habit and defensiveness which have interfered with our artistic and pedagogical mission—the full embrace of that elixir, music, without which, according to Nietzsche, life would not be worth living. By training and by personal good fortune the piano is my weapon, that all-purpose instrument capable of reproducing the patterns and colors of exotic rugs, rugged mountains, and mounted butterflies. Never was a man happier with this accident and metaphor of life that fell into his hands.

The subject matter of this book falls into various rough and overlapping categories. The original concept intended to approximate the process of interpretation, in the way that ideas about music come spontaneously to mind from different sources. The character of a piece, the sound of a piece, its technical execution, its antecedents, its structure all belong to a necessary continuum of thought which informs and coordinates the enterprise. Every tone has its source and message, and the finger responsible for that tone should reflect the variety of life's tempers and vignettes. That is what is meant by a cultivated tone.

Nevertheless, reason prevailed, or at least habit, reason's favorite author. Such that there are now five different sections: on piano playing, teaching, general cultural and aesthetic observations, musical scores, and finally a coda indulging the random mix originally favored. All the materials, whichever subject, are presented in short essays verging on the aphoristic, a style compatible with (1) a restless mind; (2) poetic fancy; (3) musical contingencies; (4) maxims (a teacher's self-defense); or all of the above, take your choice. Needless to say, all opinions are conditional, all theories suspect. What can be fairly represented as the authentic component of this book is mostly a function of the lifetime of practicing I have put in, of what it means to sit in front of a piano and dream, fret, rage, and give thanks.

Of opinions there is no shortage here, many of which are indeed highly opinionated and of a vehemence that, I trust, stops short of venom. For no response other than stubborn resistance and fury seems appropriate for me to the many meretricious compromises of the day. And if I vent my anger, it is because music was presented to me as the province of legends, heroes, and saints. Not least Saint George, but as well Saint Francis. Such is the life of a pianist, each piece a well, or pit, of opportunity.

I am indebted to too many people to mention most. For instance, my rhapsodies on the powers and blunders of the thumb in piano technique are greatly inspired by conversations with the wonderfully poetic pianist-pedagogue Irma Wolpe. And the contacts with older friends, such as Jacob Maxin, or newer friends, such as Katja Andy, fanned the flames by their evocations and appreciations of the great old masters of piano playing. But there are four people I must thank individually. The composer Gunther Schuller, who by the example of his extraordinary versatility and generosity so comfortably fits the mold of the Liszt of this century, has helped me in ways tangible and intangible beyond count. Rudolf Kolisch, dearest friend of my teacher, gave me sunshine and icicles, the hard facts and tender vows of music, which he radiated to the core and to all around him. Then there is my teacher, Edward Steuermann, whom I recall lovingly throughout the book. I was eleven years old when I came to him. It is very simple to say: without him I would not be a musician; without him I would not be a person of any serious intent or content. And then there is my wife. Without her I would not be.

THE GAME

To play the piano is to consort with nature. Every mollusk, galaxy, vapor, or viper, as well the sweet incense of love's distraction, is within the hands and grasp of the pianist. The result may be a mess or a blessing, but too often resembles a de facto hand-me-down, a vestigial imitation, a weary if wily synthetic.

𝄽

Sound is the ether which sustains and infuses the universe. But not the one isolated sound, always groupings

and multiples of sound. A single sound is but a vanity, a
betrayal of communion and community. The presumed
beauty of a single tone is rather like Helen without Troy:
a narcotic without dreams. Before the invention of ecology
there was merely consort: a calculus of variegated sonorities
in a four-dimensional phase, a topological dance choreographed by Balanchine but in sound.

𝄽

When the shepherd sings, the earth moans, the wind
murmurs, the aspen trembles. Each refrain is but a response
to a chorale audible only to Schumann's elect, to the better
and silent portion of human character. When Artur Schnabel said that he played the rests, if not the notes, better
than other pianists, he was acknowledging that subliminal
choir only silence can reveal.

𝄽

Cantabile is the cartilage connecting any two sounds,
whether made by bone or braying. It is the silken fiber which
binds two grains, two islands, two exiles. It is the urge to
fathom, to accept, to exonerate the alien gasps of mistrust,
the lonely pleas, the harsh deeds, the frigid icons. It is the
necklace and DNA of the chain of being. It is, according to
Beethoven, the most important thing in piano playing.

𝄽

By itself even the sweetest tuned tone is an aberration.
Beautiful tone, the adornment of our profession, is ultimately a narcissistic void. There are only tones, tones to be
gathered like berries or shells, and to be strung together
after scrupulous investigation of the chemistry of shells and
berries and of their mating habits. And how do shells and
berries mate? Listen to the left hand in recordings by Rachmaninoff, to the network of responsiveness it authors and
its relationship to the melody.

℔

A tone is beautiful only in context. Or as Edward Steichen pointed out, in the first stage of photography one is interested exclusively in the foreground tree. In the next stage, the surrounding shrubs and grasses become the focal point. Then finally we turn back to the tree, but within the dynamic of reciprocal planes. The conductor Charles Munch once said that the reason God gave us two ears was so that what goes in one may go out the other. God also gave us two hands. What one reports, the other retorts.

℔

Each hand has two parts, in dire and direct opposition. Thus the thumb works against the fingers, creating two prongs which form a flexing claw to explore the spectrum of sound. But most pianists play with one hand, all quarters falling into an amorphous and garbled blend of sound, whether smooth or coarse. A minority play with two hands, approximating the zones of high and low. A few elect to play with four hands, the thumbs like horns and violas. The effect can be like spinning objects in curved space, near and far, the fixed poles of illusion and reality dissembled, disarmed, and disarming.

℔

John Constable observed that the art of reading nature is no less "acquired" than the art of reading hieroglyphics. To grasp and delineate the relationship between melody and bass is no less elusive. One may speculate that the topic of free will versus predestination should be thoroughly researched (or splendidly intuited) before melody and bass, the surrogates for fantasy and fate, can be properly matched. Therefore, the logical starting point for the education of a pianist might well be the study of Greek tragedy.

℔

The idea of technique is consistently misunderstood. People think that piano technique is a matter of double thirds, fast octaves, and such specialized tricks, analogous to the current debasement of figure skating into nothing more than a series of triple axels and toe loops separated by long intervals of coasting and prayer. Technique, like poetry, is but handmaiden to the music, and should be entirely at the service of the imagination. Without imagination there is no technique, only facility. Catching a sound, like catching a fish, is a function not of physical prowess but of the hand's sensitivity in gauging the currents and resistance of the musical flow.

ọ̀

The hand must be supple. As the Navajo tradition advises, we should move through space with the lightness of a hummingbird. But as the athletes counsel, our actions, our motions must begin with the larger muscles of the torso, with the legs and the back. The balance and buoyancy which can derive only from the back's support is a necessary precondition to the flexibility of the hand. The hand may caress only because the back sustains. The resulting lightness of hand expresses itself through the reciprocal oscillation of thumb and fingers, which may vibrate as rapidly as the wings of a bird or as slowly as the arms of a Balinese dancer.

ọ̀

To know the piano is to know the universe. To master the piano is to master the universe. The spectrum of piano sound acts as a prism through which all musical and nonmusical sounds may be filtered. The grunts of sheep, the braying of mules, the popping of champagne corks, the sighs of unrequited love, not to mention the full lexicon of sounds available to all other instruments—including whistles, scrapes, bleatings, caresses, thuds, hoots, plus sweet and sour pluckings—fall within the sovereignty of this most bare and dissembling chameleon.

ò

To succeed as a pianist, one's intelligence quotient should reside on either of two distinct levels: an I.Q. of below 110 or above 140. The lively curiosity which distinguishes those who are in between will militate against the focused tenacity required to play the piano and to master its physical and structural labyrinths. It is like looking at Mars through a telescope for six hours each day while tracing the Byzantine network of its grooves and clusters, lines and patterns. One has to be a little inhuman or insane, stupid or brilliant.

ò

The thumb is the capital, the fingers are the provinces. The fingers pay taxes to the thumb, which in turn diminishes the taxing strain on the fingers by providing a general security system and command center. The thumb is an ultra-benevolent despot except in times of war, when it marshals its retinue of howitzers and torpedoes, of which it has the greatest supply. Then everybody is grateful to have such a strong boss. But otherwise, when the loudest sonorities are the chirping of cicadas or the mating rites of bees with flowers, the thumb becomes the invisible (if not inaudible) branch to the filigree of fingers.

ò

A recent scientific study has determined that fifty-seven percent of people who play the piano with curved fingers have curved noses, while sixty-three percent who employ flat fingers have decidedly flat noses. There seems to be an anatomical motif which precedes any choice of technical methods. One wonders about similar correlations with other parts of the body, but so far only one other cogent study has emerged, that of gratifying comfort to my particular lot. For, apparently, a federal research project has shown a dramatic link between falling fingers and falling arches, to both of which I can make abundant claim.

In other words, some do and some don't. Technique is finally a matter of perpetual adjustments and compensations.

𝆑

It is reported that the great golfer Ben Hogan once said that the first time a person swings a golf club one can be sure that everything he is doing is wrong. This suggests that the proper golf stroke may be far more complicated and arcane than the correct action for striking a piano key, although a more likely explanation may lie in the fact that we usually take up golf at a much later age than when we first learn the piano. The appropriate coordination for playing the piano might seem equally baffling if one began in one's thirties. In fact there are remarkable parallels between golf and piano in their mutual need for disciplined introspection. Assuredly, both have the same capacity for provoking miserable frustration.

𝆑

The definition of piano playing by Ambrose Bierce remains unchallenged: a method of producing sound by simultaneously depressing the keys and the spirits of the audience. The piano is a box, a machine, a neutral Goliath which can never respond to prosaic ways of expressing affection. The piano must be seduced by gestures that are ineffably subtle, indirect, insinuating, filmy, and delicate. The carriage of a pianist must express a noble and congruous vision disguising discrete, incongruent motions and shards melted to form a mirror of luminous sound. The stroke must be infinitely pliant, resilient, and perpetually self-correcting. Innumerable threads of voicing and texture must be merged into a single prism of sound, reflecting the plasticity of both player and music.

ọ

The thumb is not only the pivot and navigator of the hand; it is also the anchor, the Moor, the mooring, and the grey eminence, the catalyst, carburetor, conductor, tax collector, toxin, and jury, the fool and pillar, the pillow and support, the dumpling, furnace, and probe, the repository of memory and strategy, the compass, boundary, bounder, and lazy vagabond. Dinu Lipatti devised legato scales for the thumb to refine its coarse nature while Claudio Arrau blessed it for its powers of memory. The thumb is by birth a beast on the way to becoming an aristocrat.

ọ

Body motions are circular and synergistic: the energy flows in both directions. When the fingertip strikes the key, at the apex of the yield (but a yield mediated by the demands of taste), the sound is grasped, stored, and parceled for return to the heart and hearth of the spinal spring, where it is then absorbed and refurbished for the next round-trip. Of course there is considerable traffic along the way, with many impulses passing back and forth through the system. But the merest flicker of a *pianissimo* has both its genesis and demise in the broadest regions of our anatomy, of our consciousness.

ọ

The hand should be quiet, tranquil, floating. It is supported by the spine, whose stable strength is cantilevered through the shoulders and elbows, which, in turn, support the weightless and buoyant hand at rest. But in motion the hand channels the torso's energy, echoing and concentrating the body's disposition, the heart's disposition toward contraction and release. So that when the third finger, for example, presses the key down, the thumb and palm are reciprocally activated; both gently cruise toward the upper phalanx of fingers as the hand closes, stimulating and pressuring the third finger to yield its sound, then sustaining and cushioning the impact as the cycle reverses and the hand reopens.

φ

The palm (led by the thumb) and the grouped squadron of four fingers are as two Spanish dancers in a game of mutual attraction and repulsion. What happens on one side has an immediate and catalyzing effect on the other. A continuous cycle binds the partners in an exchange whose fervor depends upon the character of sound desired. The hinge which separates and fuels the exchange is located at the ridge of the top row of knuckles. The angle formed by the two segments fusing at this ridge will be flatter or steeper according to the degree of flexion in the hand. In the crisis of striking the key, the angle is sharper; when the hand is at rest, the angle is flatter.

φ

Irrespective of activity or quiet, the bond between both sides of the hand is never interrupted. As in Siamese twins, the communication is predestined and constant, such that the most subtle intimations are sufficient to confirm the link. Thus, the hand may be overtly at rest, tranquil, and composed to the observing eye, but within it a steady stream of neurons, chatter, and beneficent greetings pass through its cleft halves, back and forth, then up through the arm and shoulder to the back, then returning again to the hand, where the quiet (or ferocious) embrace of this consuming claw eats and digests the tones. Even in sleep the digestive process never stops.

⍣

The second finger has many guises in real life. It is the index finger, the trigger finger, and the finger which beckons. All these roles are absorbed into its pianistic functions, for it has considerable responsibilities: to keep order, to navigate, to set up. As the squad leader juxtaposed against the thumb, it has the awesome task of serving as liaison between Cyclops and the maidens, entities of radically different lineage and voice. It must cooperate with both sides to harmonize the differences, and as such it develops a distinctively androgynous personality, capable of both soothing the beast and regulating the bevy. It is the finger which may require the most care and attention.

⍣

The second finger, as index and forefinger, must lead the way. Poised at the inner boundary of both sides, it serves as foreman of a search party in conjunction with both the thumb and the pinky to explore the keyboard and identify the fixed (but displacing) positions. In carrying out this assignment, the thumb and second finger develop a healthy mutual respect which exhibits itself by the halo they form when touching tips, indicative of the supple tension that binds and distinguishes them. In addition, and vitally important, the index finger provides base, compass, and support for the otherwise tender pinky, which desperately needs healing and hardening to accomplish its painfully exposed mission as guardian of the melody line.

⍣

The third finger borders on being a fraud. It elicits the disgust of many pianists, who would gladly exchange theirs if L. L. Bean offered a suitable replacement. As the tallest fellow, it suggests strength, which occasionally it delivers. Yet it imagines itself to be the center axis of the hand, a total delusion, believing therefore it deserves property rights and comparable allegiance. But a portrait of Chopin's hand testifies that the center is closer to the second rather than the third finger, evidence of the hand's inherent duality of structure. Worst of all, the third finger does not react precisely to rhythmic cues; it is clearly sluggish and out of breath after a certain period, and is coordinated more like a clown on stilts than a Watusi warrior. Pay little attention to it, for it only confounds and can never be fully rehabilitated.

𝕢

Traditionally and physiologically, the fourth finger is considered the weak sister. Everyone knows that it is feeble and fragile, unfocused in its attack, unsure of its landing. It refuses to emerge from its dependence upon the third finger, to the mutual confusion of both. Artificial devices, such as Schumann's contraption to liberate it, result only in frustration or trauma. We keep trying, yet it seems hopeless. But wait! Chopin designates the fourth finger for crucial missions of the *cantabile* touch. Incredible, for we have been on the wrong track all these years. Instead of trying to mechanize it, we should be honoring its special gift. For what we thought was a one-legged flamingo may turn out to be a bird of paradise!

𝕢

It always seems that the pinky is more pink than plucky, and makes a sound more plinky than pellucid. Dear Arthur Rubinstein, from which Muse did you order your statuesque pinky? It's really not fair to be a mere mortal, to have but a normal pinky that reaches only to the second knuckle of the fourth finger. But let us think it through. For the weakness of the pinky may reside not in its shortness but rather in our fear that it is short and weak. So that we grab prematurely for the top note (which distills the lyrical essence), or in fact for the low note (the voice of authority). Conclusion: slow down the action of the pinky and the move to the outside. Take time, but also use the thumb and forefinger as guide and pillar for the fifth finger. Triangulate the target and buttress the support.

𝄢

The posture is complete. The spine is long, gently arched, extending like a tower from the small of the back to the base of the skull. The legs are calm but free. The energy travels from the soles of the feet (which control the pedals, the "soul of the piano") through the legs to the spine. The shoulders are sloping, like those of Joe Di-Maggio and other great athletes, and are suspended from the spine with the elbows hanging gently away from the torso. Circulation is all. The wrist is lower than the ridge at the top of the knuckles, never depriving the hand of full extension for its opening and closing ceremony. Breathing, distribution, equilibrium, flexibility, the attitude of a panther ready to spring, of a moth floating in air.

𝄢

Each gesture is known by its opposite. Recuperation, resilience, rebound, the finger striking and releasing with equal impetus. Martha Argerich once told a student of mine to practice with the fingers moving *upward*, as though the keyboard were above the hand, not below it. A fanciful image of a practical truth. Our way of characterizing the next note is based upon our estimate of the note preceding. How we recall, recoup, recover from the previous sounds will be the guide to those forthcoming. Thus the quality of ingestion is crucial to the plans for execution. The body is a sympathetic membrane, for hearing, processing, and delivering the skein of sound. To abet the process, we do not relax as such—a rather tired panacea. Instead we listen, we disappear, we are reborn, a continuous pulse of creation. Alertness, which is passive fire.

ọ̀

The club head is at rest, directly behind the ball, before the swing is initiated. The golfer addresses the ball. The direction, strength, and character of the shot are rehearsed and visualized before the golfer springs into action. In strictly analogous fashion, the pianist addresses the keyboard. The finger is prepared, directly over the key, before the stroke begins. The dynamic, timing, and quality of the sound are vividly conceptualized before the finger descends to make its fateful choice. There are two preliminary stages interlocking: conception and preparation. Absent one or the other, the game is lost.

ọ̀

The thumb is a finger in the sense that a whale is a fish. This grand illusion is perpetuated by mountains of exercises designed to domesticate the lazy leviathan, the wild boar, the black sheep who is forbidden to roam on the black keys. So we coddle, cradle, and seduce the beast to behave like a mama's boy, and would consider either total banishment (as in the old days) or symbolic operation to soften its gender. But you cannot make a silk purse out of a sow's ear. Don't put a tutu on the piggy. Take advantage of his friendly and vigorous snout, which goes right to the kernel and core of the matter, to the stabilizing of the hand position.

ọ̀

Without the opposable thumb, the hand would scratch and feed like that of our monkey cousins. The sibling second through fifth fingers form a phalanx working against the thumb, four against one, but it's a battle that ends in a draw. As the two segments attract and repel, so the hand opens and closes, contracts and releases, analogous to the basic exercises of the body folding and unfolding, as devised by Martha Graham. Tension concentrating and dissipating, the story of man, fate, and all cycles. The hand opens, the hand closes, from which alternation come trills, tremolos, and articulated energy. Everything graceful and good that flows from the hand begins in this machine with two pistons in contrary motion.

ϱ

Five fingers uniformly independent and efficient. According to the model of Liszt, ten fingers equivalent and continuous, belonging to one master hand. The fingers become extensions of the brain, the ear; they exist only as conduits of imagined sound. They are agents and servants, lasers and radiants of the bequeathing mind, which conjures the universe as a slide show of sounds in varied colors and designs. They are selfless. They are neutral. But, unfortunately, even monastic discipline does not render them immune to nicks, cuts, warts, tendinitis, and brain distemper.

ϱ

Five fingers wholly dissimilar in their function and effect. Each one, according to Chopin, singular in weight and gift, and to be prized for its selective attributes. So that the ultimate texture of sound is produced by the wise distribution of disparate weights and timbres, creating a tableau of lighter or denser sonorities which reveals the shifting, multidimensional imagery. Curses on this assortment of wayward, unkempt, ill-matched toy soldiers! No, to the contrary! Blessings to this hand of exquisitely discriminating and complementary conspirators, who divide the labor as skillfully as a gang of bank robbers.

ϱ

The fingertip is animate flesh. The piano key is inanimate solid, formerly porous ivory, now seamless plastic. The breath, prayers, and libido of the fingertip must somehow be transferred to the neutral indifference of the key. The poor pianist: first he must overcome all his own psychic indispositions, and then he must charm this black box without nerves (yet thoroughly neurotic in its wayward cranks and creaks), all the while maneuvering through the glassy skin of its keys. As portrayed on the ceiling of the Sistine Chapel, the breath of life is passed on. The pianist becomes a serene immanence, the piano by extension an embodiment of spirit and grace.

♩

The fingertip sinks into the key, secure but free. The entire apparatus, from tip to toe, through the arms, torso, and legs, hangs gently off the nexus between flesh and key. The motion is up and down, north and south, lined up on the axis formed by key, finger, and elbow. The fingertip adheres possessively (but tenderly) to the key, like a child suckling, like a monkey swinging off a branch firmly grasped by its limb or tail. The contact is sealed, flowing, momentarily eternal.

♩

The vow between fingertip and key must be channeled, churned, filtered, distributed to the receptors and shock absorbers of the body. The moment of assignation between flesh and key is both shock and release, requiring the intervention of every part of the anatomy. The body absorbs the shock; it assimilates the message of the sound; it reviews the evidence and relays instructions for the next sound. The body is a sounding board, a switchboard, a comfort station, a generator for the troops on line, the fingertips. These troops are well regulated and serve every spectrum of the personality—and the music.

♩

Timing is all. But premature relationships turn out to be shallow. If the equation between impact and absorption is too facile, too quick, the tone will neither sing nor project. That is why Madame Isabella Vengerova, formerly of the Curtis School, insisted upon exercising the fingertips for several years, urging them to sink deeply into the keys through the lowering and raising of the wrist, again and again, to develop resiliency and toughness. Until this side of the equation matures, the larger body frame will not have an appropriate partner or challenge. And the sound will be pale, even if fleet or flashy.

ȹ

It is clear that there is a circuit, a symbiosis between fingertip and frame, as though they were figure and ground, tree and shrub, plus sun. Nor can one determine which side initiates the process. For the fingertip has memory, the memory has touch, and the body embraces all dimensions of touch and conception. The trick is to incorporate the neutral key into this eternal triangle, and to make three into one—something like Tinker to Evers to Chance, who executed the double play with such singular ease.

ȹ

To perfect this sleight of hand, shell game, and integrated circuitry demands a certain style, a certain grace to weave one out of many. The visual abstract is represented by a circle, without beginning or end and with tracks running in both directions, so that the impulse, sound content, and energy may flow both in unison and counterpoint. Put simply, the piano and the pianist mate. But the pianist, poor human, is both mind and matter. Perhaps, then, it is the piano which tempers the split, which mends the rupture, which closes the circle. Perhaps the piano is the ideal therapist for human ails, breaches, and distress.

ȹ

Ontogeny recapitulates phylogeny. The human organism embraces the history of its evolutionary ancestors. The hu-

18 { · Russell Sherman · }

man hand echoes the manifold talents of animal limbs, from slithering to rending. Every gesture of our hand at the piano is indebted to the memory and model of some animal's magical properties of motion and locomotion. When our playing is dead, dry, dehydrated, dogmatic, or dormant, it is often because we have forgotten our ancestors.

♢

When one hears golfers rhapsodizing over the ingredients of the perfect swing, the subtleties and intricacies of their art seem far more formidable than the mundane tasks of the pianist. For the golfer, the body language is incredibly fine-tuned, requiring (1) a flowing but strictly profiled function of the various parts (for instance, the right elbow tucked quite unnaturally into the side of the torso); and (2) an exquisitely timed, precise coordination of all the differentiated elements of the stroke.

What is repeatedly emphasized, however, is the role of the legs in both balancing and propelling the swing. The incantations of Jack Nicklaus, acknowledged as the supreme shotmaker, on the legs' contribution to power and balance are instructive to both neutral observer and pianist. For the legs initiate the stroke; the legs cushion the tensions of both stroke and nerves; the legs begin and close the cycle of physical coordination; the grounding of the feet reinforces the sensation of stability and its counterpart, soaring. Add to these factors that the pianist's feet are responsible for the pedals, the stairway to heaven.

♢

Another precept of Jack Nicklaus advises that the swing cannot move any faster than the feet can regulate. Now what does this have to do with piano playing?

Despite the many technical skills which have prospered in recent years, the quality of pedal control has declined dramatically. The pedal should be the great arbiter of tonal chemistry, with the ability to mix long and short, loud and soft notes into varieties of malleable texture. This requires a calibrated flexibility in the use of the damper pedal, which is able to respond to the multiple personae of the musical image, in durations and dimensions from the fleeting to the sustained. For this to happen the foot must be as sensitive as the hummingbird's wings, as the suitor's heart.

♩

The pedal spectrum is like an unexplored continent, a lost Atlantis, a potential paradise of illusion and despair. It harbors such color possibilities as are found in the realms of sensual, psychological play that Gauguin portrayed in his Tahitian chronicle. That is, it evokes the grave, the magical, the luminous. In practice we use it like an appliance, like a washing machine or vacuum cleaner, on or off. Thick sound/dry sound, flood/drought, suet/straw, barren of choice and destitute of image—indeed a Hobson's choice of the nearest gel or nothing at all.

♩

The hand is structured; the hand is fluid. Both paradigms are true, and both coexist; but they must be individually addressed before their ultimate integration.

The sequence of development typically proceeds as follows: (1) the child's hand is initially resilient, spongy, amorphous; (2) some degree of structure and conformation is imposed, if only by way of analogy to patterns of meter and mode; (3) after the hand has developed an "appropriate" position capable of clarifying and controlling the notes, the demands of expression and virtuosity require some loosening of the outer mold. Nevertheless, while flexibility is vital, it should not subvert a basic concept of profile and organization.

As in every athletic activity, there is a continuous dynamic embracing both static and moving components. The contemporary love affair with viscous fluidity, activated against the demonic pariah of tension, is no less exaggerated than an earlier model of the hand so rigid that it could support a dime on its back while in motion.

Tension: the great bugaboo, bit, and gulag of enlightened folk. On the other side, for rejecting loose indulgence and all its languorous dissipations, there is the law-and-order constabulary (but now in eclipse). In the middle is the poor piano student, set adrift by the current apostles of free ride, free fall, free lunch, all blessed with a shot of Zen.

There are certain things, however, to keep in mind. Zen serendipity, legitimately admired, is yet based upon a highly structured regimen which does not allow for random choice (or non-choice) until all aspects and all possible solutions to a problem have been exhausted. Moral: when one knows the notes, the rhythms, the passages, and the memory inside out under strict control procedures, only then is freedom eminently desirable.

Piano playing, however uniquely invested with a multitude of human and superhuman implications, is still but another variety of muscular exertion. A careful analysis of other (and in the physical sense no less complicated) athletic activities illustrates, as in Zeno's paradox, a character of motion which is both continuous and incremental—proceeding from station to station. Without locating the stations, the motion deteriorates to anarchy, however attractively choreographed.

♩

For example, in a golfer's swing there are numerous checkpoints along the way, identified as essential to trace the path of the swing and to ensure maximum control and leverage. It is exactly the same whether stroking a ball, pitching a ball, swinging a bat, or doing a pirouette. But in piano playing we are rather drunk with the ideal of unencumbered, frictionless motion as an antidote to any whiff of tension, motivated perhaps by the burden of dealing with so many notated variables. Since the score is always changing and the notes seem to run amok in all directions, we feel we have to be infinitely adaptable—to some mythical point where the hands can be trusted to accomplish what our brains are too slow to manage.

Trust your brain, my teacher would say. For the volatile patterns of notes must be organized into tangible as well musical compartments. The hand moves in discrete gestures from place to place as a bird moves from branch to branch—elegantly but purposefully, unrushed but undaunted, smoothly and economically. The musical content is divided into corresponding physical increments which the hand charts, pursues, and gathers. The results of entirely unpunctuated motion, however, would end up rather like a bird slamming into a plate-glass window.

How does the hand look as it moves from point to point? Does it flip, does it smile, does it coil or uncoil, flutter, freeze, dart, dangle? I suggest that it moves rather quietly, an unobtrusive guest, a wary pickpocket, a sly adventurer. But it retains always a certain poise, a certain bearing and carriage, a certain *je ne sais quoi*. Nor does it ever forget its primordial debt to the opposable thumb. Two antennae in pursuit of delicious prey.

♩

The exchange between the thumb and brother phalanx (Cain and Abel) transpires within the condition and context of perpetual pliancy. The motion, the range, the power issue from a current operating between the two separate gen-

erating stations, contrary but coexisting. The hand moves
in one piece carried from aloft, but walking, scurrying,
floating on its two fangs. The hand is carried by the fore-
arm, hanging gently from the elbow from the shoulder
from the neck from the spine from the hips from the legs
from the feet. All the different parts are intricately meshed,
geared, and socketed reciprocally, one into the other in a
circuit which is source, cushion, platform to the stroke of
the hand. The wrist has a more equivocal function, congruent to the other parts but primarily as an agent of trans-
mission. It is the open valve which allows the larger
anatomy to participate fully.

Movement and structure, flow and frame are partners
forever pledged and bound.

Ι

The imperatives of *cantabile*, the sine qua non of musical
expression and piano playing, demand a clear segregation
of the various planes of sound and discourse—into models
of foreground and background, melody and accompaniment, song and choir, poet and landscape, right hand and
left hand. Some years ago an intelligent if inexperienced
student, whom I worked with briefly at a summer camp,
put it very nicely: "dream and reality." Such was his prescription for distinguishing the basic functions of the sonority universe. The background is dense with complicated
tasks and roles, though often light in texture. Often it is
the more difficult voice to untangle and execute. For it
must provide continuity, coordinates, and a continuum of
sustaining sound to support the predilections of the solo
voice. The melody rambles and rages according to the shape
of its line and as the personality of both piece and player
warrants. Its refinements are ever challenging yet in some
sense finite, if only because its many gradations of nuance,

tone color, and phrasing are but variations of its singular ego and identity.

My own tendency is to teach the left hand first. Before the poet can sing there must be a ground, a context to locate and identify him. Otherwise he is likely to sing only about his troubles, which tend to be a rather monotonous subject.

𝄞

A persuasive *cantabile* must combine, among other things, two rather conflicting psychic components, pride and sensitivity. One need not (cannot) define sensitivity except to point out the obvious—that the musician must respond to all shadings, inflections, and shapes, to all nuances, articulations, colors, dynamics, and signs, to all the minutest indications of meaning out of respect for the wonders and feelings of the line.

As for pride, a different spirit of diction is required. Somehow there must be an attitude of secure dignity which does not stoop to pander, to indulge every morsel of melancholy or every turn of flippancy. The separate groans of lament and grains of mischief are "sensitively" embraced, yet gathered into a skein of noble declamation which reflects multiple kinds of joy: the proud joy of being a musician, the somber joy of being responsible for charting the griefs and hopes of humanity, the pleasurable joy of describing a garden of infinite colors and designs.

𝄞

To cultivate an appropriate *legato cantabile* requires three different sonic perspectives, which overlap yet contradict one another. Each is indispensable but meaningless without the others.

First, each successive note of the line must emerge from that portion of sound still lingering from the previous note.

Given the acoustical properties (liabilities) of the instrument, the sound will always decay in a rather straight line from impact to extinction, or until the next note is struck. Nevertheless the dynamic of the new tone should match the *remainder* of the previous tone, thus ensuring the smoothest possible transition. Inevitably, strict observance of this rule leads to a progressive and impractical *diminuendo*. Second, the color and quality of each note should possess the *same* character and dynamic, as though all were drawn from the same well, fired from the same crucible. But this would lead to a perpetually static, unvarying dynamic, therefore a monotone afflicting the entire line.

Third, the hierarchy of values given, as defined by contour, duration, articulation, motivic significance, and all aspects of notation, requires a constant *variation* of touch affecting the specific timbre of each tone. Thus the personality of the line is revealed. Smoothness, consistency, and variety are the fundamental and contrary ingredients of the *legato* line.

ọ

As Artur Schnabel observed, the violin and the oboe intrinsically have more characteristic sonorities than the piano. But one cannot sound like the other, and only the piano can mimic both.

The general public and the typical performer make much of pianos which have a beautiful tone. It is interesting to note, however, that two of the most idiosyncratic and fertile of recent pianists, Glenn Gould and Sviatoslav Richter, preferred to play on Yamahas, presumably for their more neutral tone and evenness upon which the artists could inscribe their individual personalities.

The glory of the piano resides in its protean flexibility. It can do anything or be anything; it can resemble the voice of rogue, saint, Aeolus, Ondine; or thrush, hummingbird, jackhammer, harlequin, coquette, or Napoléon. However, none of these voices could be summoned up unless the core sound of the piano were white, mother of all colors. Only chaste white (or sober grey) can conceal and contain such a voluptuous, turbulent mix.

When the tone is too beautiful, one becomes its prisoner.

ǫ

The inherent neutrality of the piano tone is the negative gift which permits it to be plied and sculpted in ways as diverse as the imagination can fathom. All great and trembling creatures of the sea and air are prey to the grey ambush of this nameless sound—that is, its single-minded and unsingular tone. But put two tones together, and the possibilities multiply. Put the appropriate pedal to the two tones, and vapor, fire, or famine can be invoked. If aimless beauty itself be the goal of the text, whether at the behest of sirens, dreams, or heather, there are many alchemical touches and tactics on call.

By analogy, the melodic motives in works of Beethoven do not typically have the haunting contours of melodies by Schubert or Mahler. Yes, there are some which have such poignant outlines, but in general Beethoven's melodies are divisible, a priori, into cryptic, detachable motives which become the breeding ground for future development. The range of developmental activity is directly conditioned by the relative neutrality (or starkness) of these motivic cells.

The range of the piano's gift for metaphor and metamorphosis is directly linked to its "undistinctive" sound.

ǫ

Composers are more creative, mystics more spiritual, decathlon champions more athletic, mathematicians more ingenious, mothers more heartfelt than any pianist. Of course some pianists are composers, or mystics, or mathematicians, or mothers. None is all of the above, but each one who is a legitimate member of the piano guild must be acutely gifted in all these different areas. And more, the pianist must have the presence of an actor and the passion of a prophet.

In the sense of combining all faculties of the human personality, no discipline requires more versatility and more extensive training. The proof is twofold: (1) with a few notable and isolated exceptions, no theatrical situation other than the piano recital depends exclusively upon the contributions of a single, unattended individual, alone responsible for turning the theater into a chamber of illusion; (2) comparable to the creative professions, and by some evidence in even more pronounced fashion, pianists often become better with age, as demonstrated by the recent examples of Arthur Rubinstein, Vladimir Horowitz, and Claudio Arrau. The recital of Mieczyslaw Horszowski in Carnegie Hall at the age of ninety-seven (and his later appearances!) provokes special wonder.

It is a long, bewildering, and gratifying odyssey.

♩

The pianist has two crosses to bear. The first is a practical concern, the troublesome, demoralizing, fretful struggle of earning a living, an onerous task within a culture that covets celebrity, regards classical music as elegant decor, and provides a minimum number of opportunities for the expensively trained and excess talent. When a piano position becomes available at a respectable university, two hundred respectable pianists are waiting to apply.

The other cross is of equal burden, but our Dostoyevskian souls welcome the trial. For the repertoire composed for the instrument—solo, concerto, chamber—is so infi-

nitely splendid and so splendidly infinite that we would
need a dozen lifetimes to command a substantial fraction
of the whole. We move through it like snails, consuming
more than our brains can carry and cursing those fortunate
devils blessed with photographic memory. We stagger under the weight, unsure if it is nails or elixir penetrating
our pores. It is a blessed disease. Each chapter of the struggle tempers the mind and mines the temper. We are exhausted but alive.

𝄞

The resilient gestures of dance and gymnastics are beguiling to both teacher and student looking to liberate the
physical mechanism. As always, tension is the cruel demon
which dams up the flows of springing, of springtime, of
letting the music go. It is a healthy instinct, this urge to
spring. We want the notes to describe soaring arcs, and,
more, we want to soar ourselves. The musical phrase does
not split into rigid compartments; why should our hands
move from zone to zone in frigid, discrete steps?

Then one looks at the hands of great masters. Are they
bouncing in choreographic delight as they make their way
through the intricate passages or the *largo cantabile*? Are
they tracing a path from elevated heights to keybed like
graceful parachutes, like seabirds diving and rising with
their catch?

One wants to fly, to soar, to dream and dance the night
away. It is a nice thought, a redeeming thought, and one
wishes we could play in that seamlessly elastic way. But
the masters do not oblige. In profile their hands are more
like sentries, like hawks. Their fingers prepare and probe
the notes as a cobra's fangs magnetically seek their victim.
Behind the scene the arms and torsos and legs coil and
recoil like the cobra's body. The sentries patrol; the finger-

tips breathe; safely inside the dance goes on. The music dances.

♩

There is only one law of piano playing, but it is not really a law, more the condition and premise to all the other minor statutes. It is the law of ambush. If you want to trap an elusive sixteenth note, wait in readiness and target your quarry before you pounce. Preparation is the name of the game, and without it the game has neither rules nor runs nor scores nor sounds worth praising. Readiness is the key, and as the coaches advise, visualize (or, in this case, audibilize) your target before you strike.

Readiness is not a state of tension; it is a state of alertness. The mind and body are tuned in together, chanting a quiet prelude of physical and aural vibration which acts as both image and bridge to the deed. The vibrations of this prelude are visibly gentle, assuring open passageways to the large muscles and palpable contact between anticipation and act.

But the emphatic point to be made is that the hitman or strokelady should be in the immediate vicinity of the target, in fact with their nose right in the belly of the key, or variations thereof. This kind of economy of motion is but an expression of elegance, in the sense that the arabesques which dancers trace by the design of their movements do not have time or tolerance for casual loops.

♩

The interesting and captivating memoir *The Art of Archery*, by Eugen Herrigel, was published in the vanguard of the useful, therapeutic Zen craze. In its bracing narrative of a Westerner who tried to accommodate his pragmatic ways to an ancient Japanese tradition which fostered the spiritual values of "aimlessness," there nevertheless lurk the seeds of a possible misunderstanding.

One hits the target, so the tradition declares, by "letting go," by *not* aiming. Here the mischief ensues. For letting go does not mean the careless rapture of unaccountability, of an uninhibited loosening which guarantees striking the target because the subject is purged of ambition.

It is true that the Zen master could hit the target with his eyes closed, but *only* after a studied and severe discipline had tempered him to a stage of perfect readiness. For many months the Westerner was not even permitted to shoot the arrow. First he had to learn to draw the bow, to hold it firmly in drawn position until his muscles ached, and to stand serenely in balance until the frame of his body could provide harmonious support. In a word, he had to be prepared, with all the components of mind and body participating in the colloquium of concentration.

You don't just let it all hang out, unless you gain some special pleasure from playing the buffoon.

♭

Heraclitus said that you can never step in the same river twice, a chilling insight into the evanescence of all things. But even the flow of water abides by certain principles, an illustration of the more comforting perception that chaos itself has laws.

The spontaneity of Artur Schnabel or of Thelonious Monk does not flow from unrehearsed consciousness, or because they never thought about things. It flows because they thought about things so hard and honestly that they were attuned to the puzzles and contradictions which demand a leap of faith, or play. Only from a thorough preparation which teaches all and the limitations of all can the conditions arise for inspired "accidents." Only the anguish and amusements of hard work can train one to perceive the charms of chaos, the dynamics of its properties and improprieties.

Keep your finger near the key and your mind on the sound. The image of the imminent sound, wrapped in the vision of the whole, motivates and catalyzes the body, which sways serenely before uncoiling through the hand. The character of the finger's stroke depends entirely upon the desired sound—darting, rolling, singing, singeing, stately—whatever is necessary. Praying at the altar of the sound requires quiet attentiveness and solemn preparation. Only from this stance can genuine playfulness occur.

𝄽

Without conceptualization of the desired image, there is no image; it cannot materialize despite good intentions. This is why there is no substitute for slow practicing, or "pre-practicing," without which the execution of the notes at full tempo, by virtue of one's pattern of bias and habit, could prejudice the artistic standard.

The philosopher Benedetto Croce pointed out that many people with artistic pretensions feel cheated because fate did not provide those conditions for proper study and technical development which could have enabled them to realize the splendor of their visions. For Croce this lament was but a consoling rationalization, masking conceptual inadequacies rather than technical deficiencies. If in fact a person can hear within the appropriate sounds, he will somehow find a way to produce them, and his technique will develop to the level required.

Vladimir Ashkenazy may have had something similar in mind when he remarked that technique was but a function of rhythm. Unless one can audibilize the precise durations, the fingers will cramp and fumble.

Of course, it is also nice to have light fingers and the right genes.

𝄽

In every physical act demanding grace and coordination, some parts of the body remain stable while other parts are moving. Motion must rotate, uncoil, or swing against a support column, or within a frame of relatively fixed poles. The right-handed baseball pitcher flings his arm and momentum around the stable axis provided by his left leg. Whatever pitch he throws, he is trained to plant his left leg in exactly the same spot and in exactly the same way. Without the secure grounding of this stationary axis, he cannot exploit the full range of motion and resource available for any controlled, focused gesture. Similarly, the golfer's swing rotates around the secure pole established by a firm left side, without which the swing would collapse in spasmodic disarray.

As there is no action without reaction, there is no purposeful motion without a countervailing pillar to provide resistance and reference. Something can happen only in relation to something which is not happening. Therefore the hands, arms, and torso of the pianist cannot all be flailing away in a rhapsody of release.

♩

The pianist's mechanism swings between the poles of fingertip and spine rather like a hammock. But a hammock swings from side to side, east and west, while the pianist's action is more confined to a north-south plane. It is not a matter of up and down so much, but more a coiling, rotating, almost Ferris wheel motion which transmits the contents of weight and energy in a continuous, snakelike cycle between back and fingertip. One measure of the freedom of this cycle resides in the posture of the elbow, away from the ribs while floating and bobbing on a pocket of air, lightly buoyant.

The spine should be relatively quiet, dispensing its magisterial authority with measured abundance. Everything flows into and out of the spine. It carries itself like Buddha, composed and alert. The shoulders and arms contribute their resources by riding on the wave of the spine's impulse in a gathering, gently rolling motion. The wrist moves quietly in and out like a piston. The destination is the fingertip, which lies staunchly (but flexibly) on and in the bed of the key. The fingertip absorbs and transmits the gathering momentum in one precise moment, perfectly conceived and executed.

♩

To absorb the onrush of energy from above (and below), the fingertip must be completely resilient and discriminating. It must flex on the key in such a way as to permit passage, both forward and back, of the stream of weight. And it must choose exactly the right proportion of weight to digest as decreed by the musical intentions. In its role as agent, calculator, focus, and apex of the cyclical process, the fingertip develops a nearly adhesive contact with the key, whether treading lightly or heavily. It should have the flexibility and sticking power of an orangutan's limb wound around a branch with body swinging freely. The full impact or lightest quantum of body weight must be processed with equal efficiency by the fingertip in its dual function as transmitter and rebounder of the energy supply. The fingertip should nuzzle, caress, gorge on, gambol over, press, penetrate the key, but not slide on it.

There is no rupture between stroke and rebound. As one plays the note, the recuperation already begins. Instructions for new notes and filings of old notes pass by each other along the lines of communication. The fingertip is the terminus without end or pause of this circular feedback.

♩

We live at a time which features the highest possible standards of technical execution. And we live at a time in which the culture's voracious appetite for novelty makes and breaks the careers of performing artists with reckless abandon. A glut of skilled professionals struggle for the few rungs available on the ladder of success. Meanwhile, the process of promoting one's gift is frequently exhausting, debilitating, or amoral.

No wonder then that in such a feverish environment there is a proliferation of feel-good methods designed to solace the struggling cadre of young professionals and gifted students. Prescriptions of faith and self-esteem are obvious panaceas for such dismal prospects. These counsels may be compassionate, but they are nonetheless often hollow and sad. Self-esteem is essential, but it cannot be transplanted by slogan or placebo. It can come only from steady growth fostered by guidance which is consistent, sophisticated, resourceful, and caring.

One satisfaction remains undaunted by harsh reality: the sustaining pleasures of good work. The pianist's job well done is the happiest of fates. No more compassionate message can be offered or felt.

♀

The bouncing up and down of happy hands represents the physical analogy to feel-good methods for boosting the psyche. The bogeyman here, as always, is vile tension, lean as Cassius and mean as Iago. But, in fact, how does tension develop?

Tension arises from insecurity, and insecurity arises from ignorance. Ignorance, in our line of work, means not knowing the notes—an umbrella charge covering a multitude of sins, such as not knowing how the notes are organized, related, structured, and composed. That is, one's not knowing the *composition* leads to a good deal of insecurity even if all the tactile and mnemonic devices are functioning. Spurious gestures of liberation superimposed on a shaky foundation and insufficient grounding in the detail provide only a film of authority.

If, however, the notes are securely fastened and the mechanism is orderly, the answer lies not in the elimination of tension, for tension is the sword and glue òf music, but in the *distribution* of tension. The spine, the arms, the shoulders, the legs, the torso all must share in the musical enterprise, and by their breathing and coordination convert it into a statement of convictions. Tension, nerves, psychic and metaphysical uncertainty are in fact the actual ingredients of musical pathos if properly balanced and exploited.

ò

Of vocabulary and its variables, one may find experts in all fields. Never have I seen an athlete better in command of the variables of his game than the hockey player Wayne Gretzky. With uncanny awareness he can project the position of all players on the ice, friend or foe, where they are and where they should go, in order to make the perfect pass at the perfect speed—truly a skill of Mozartean grace. His efficiency is the measure of his knowledge of the game, its structure, its history, its nuances, its opportunities.

For instance, as pianists we could have more options of sound color by emulating the timbre and sonority of older fortepianos. The left-hand accompaniments in works of the Classical period should reflect the peculiarly limber and woodsy sound of these traditional instruments, adding a spry athleticism to the more languorous palette of modern pianos. And then, how much richness awaits our touch if we are conversant with the phenomenal expansion of the percussion section in contemporary music. The mythic so-

norities therein can inspire psychic as well acoustic reso-
nances in the music of any period.

Sound is the name for the field of our game, and we are
the players who pass the puck. But if Wayne Gretzky is
the pianist on this team, then Bobby Orr is the organist.

𝄞

There is power and there is resonance. Power is nice but
resonance is nicer. Power can be dry, nasty, aggressive. Resonance may not have power, but it is powerful. It presents
the music as a spectrum of energies, combining tones short
and long, tones light and dark, chirpy and thick, mobile
and sustained. The secret to resonance is—who knows? But
for the piano, while many factors contribute to its special
sound, there is one arbiter which reigns, but should not
pour.

The pedal is everything to the pianist, the boulevard to
his favorite café, the setting to his sun, the road to excess,
discrimination, and heaven. Everything can come from fine
and infinite uses of the pedal—above all, resonance, and in
particular that resonance which is the key to space, line,
point, and time.

Even before Albert Einstein there were four dimensions,
of which the canny and the uncanny pianist was the dis-
cerning master.

𝄞

The English say that the purpose of baseball is to hit a
round ball with a round bat squarely. The art of piano
playing is to persuade the audience that the effect of a
hammer striking wire is heavenly.

Pianos are mischievous, hybrid, mechanical elephants
whose ivories are no longer available for tickling. The limited pool of desirable pianos remaining should be preserved
by the endangered species act. The requisite materials and

craftsmanship are in short supply, vulnerable to the laws of mass production.

Several years ago a famous pianist gave a master class at our conservatory. In the discussion which followed, he was questioned about the problem of dealing with different pianos at each stop on the tour. It turns out, he answered rather whimsically, that there are exactly thirteen kinds of bad pianos in circulation. Having identified which category of inadequate instrument was furnished for the particular concert, he would simply make the necessary mental adjustments and retire to his hotel room with equanimity.

Another version of the same resigned attitude is revealed in an anecdote about Sviatoslav Richter. When invited by the concert manager to try the instrument immediately upon his arrival, Richter gratefully accepted, went to the hall, sat down at the piano, adjusted the bench, put his hands silently on the keyboard, and pronounced himself satisfied and ready to leave. When the puzzled manager inquired why Richter did not actually test the *sound* of the piano, the pianist responded, Because I am always disappointed.

♀

In fact there are good pianos, there are bad pianos, and mostly there are indifferent ones. Apart from the ingredients of mechanical action, there are four vital elements which concern the pianist: (1) the sustaining—or decay—factor of the individual notes, in particular those in the treble register; (2) the timbre or quality of the notes, both individually and in "concert"; (3) the range of dynamics available; (4) the equivalence of voicing from note to note, register to register. Many people feel that the first two factors are the vital components. I believe, however, that the characteristics of range and voicing are more significant.

Aristotle observed that range was the primary constituent of great art. Of course, he meant this as a function of dramatic, not decibel, power. But for the performing artist there is a direct if not causal relation between the two. For without the extremes of sharply contrasting dynamics, the exigencies of both plot and sonority cannot be adequately portrayed.

On the other hand, consistently even voicing is the basis for delineating precise shapes and balances of sound. And so-called beautiful, not to mention meaningful, sound is more the by-product of control than of the aesthetic qualities of individual notes. It is nice to have both, but accountability is more important than looks.

𝆕

The very concept and possibility of an intrinsically beautiful piano is somewhat of an illusion, a kind of *trompe l'oreille*. Twofold evidence punctures this illusion: pianos that may sound irresistible in the showroom or in one particular hall do not necessarily sound appealing in another location; and a good piano serviced by an inexperienced technician may quickly lose its bloom.

The moral is that the attributes of beautiful or radiant sound depend upon a troika of conditions—the instrument, the technician, the venue. Minus the contributions of any one of these factors, the character of the sound is noticeably compromised. Assuming the piano is reasonably presentable, perhaps the most significant of these conditions is the quality of the technician. A wise and subtle technician can prepare an indifferent instrument for effective use, unless the range of sound is severely restricted or the action is inordinately clumsy.

In the sense of an absolute standard covering the essential parameters, there is no such thing as an infallibly good piano (although there are many doomed pianos). But the essential equation is a good piano serviced by a good technician in a sympathetic hall.

𝜚

If there are no pianos which infallibly excel without reliable technicians in acoustically compatible halls, there are also no piano makers who uniformly produce good pianos. Some makers are better than others, but the choice of an instrument for the home or the hall based exclusively upon the pedigree of the maker is more a reflex than a choice. Everything depends upon the variables, of which the most applicable is captured by the sensible saying, Different strokes for different pieces and different kinds of music.

Generic differences between the various brands may obtain but should be regarded skeptically. To make an obvious and inviting comparison, American Steinways often have a rather warm, even voluptuous and burgundy sound. Their counterparts, the German Steinways, usually feature a more transparent, silvery, and champagne sound. Yet both have their respective disadvantages, the richness of the American palette often turning dense and immobile, the focused German sound becoming shrill. Each offers a different action, with many pianists preferring the more frictionless Hamburg version.

Of course, other piano labels have their characteristic and attractive qualities. The more the merrier, as long as we judge the instrument by its individual merits, not by its brand or advertising.

𝜚

Ideally, each hall should have two or three pianos, a different one for each style of music—for instance, a Mozart piano, a Chopin piano, and a Prokofiev piano. Ideally, a pianist whose recital program may comprise such contrasting styles should perform each work on a different piano.

For just as there is no such beauty or beast as the perfect piano, there is no such thing as the all-purpose piano.

The important thing, for player and listener, is to worry less about the piano than the performance. This was elegantly put by James Galway, who, when asked if he preferred to play on his gold flute or his platinum flute, replied with blunt candor that it didn't really matter very much —it was not the flute, it was the player that counted.

The other axiom which should not be forgotten refers to the very nature of music, its universal meanings and associations. As in all expression of art, what matters is depth, vision, and imagination. Conventional beauty comes in two sizes, skin-deep and "classical" proportions. Real beauty, as any Caucasian staring in amazement at the decorative motifs of African Masai must acknowledge, can be remarkably subjective. The piano is not born to be a purveyor of sweetness; it is an extraordinary and versatile means to mirror the world and its diverse treasures.

♭

The public fascination with paragons of technical perfection and legerdemain is not exclusive to our materialistic age. The nineteenth-century German poet and musician E.T.A. Hoffmann satirized the virtuoso type in his collection of musical essays, *Kreisleriana*. His "Letter from Milo, an educated ape, to his lady-friend Pipi in North America" delightfully parodies the charms and conceits of megatechnique.

> *You are aware, my sweet, that nature has endowed me*
> *with rather longish fingers; with these I can span*
> *fourteenths, even two octaves, and this, together with*
> *enormous skill in moving and animating my fingers, is my*
> *whole secret of fortepiano playing. My music-master shed*
> *tears of joy over the outstanding gifts of his pupil, for*
> *within a short time I reached the point where I could run*

up and down with both hands in demisemiquavers,
hemidemisemiquavers, even semihemidemisemiquavers,
without a mistake, play trills with all my fingers equally
well, and execute leaps of three or four octaves up and
down, just as I used to leap from one tree to the next. As
a result I am the greatest virtuoso there can be.

♩

Without technique there is no art. Yet technique is part of the service economy; it does not manufacture goods but facilitates their production. When technique becomes an end in itself, the result is music reduced to scales, chords, arpeggios, trills, octaves, leaps, and other tools of the piano garage. In place of musical ideas and their elaborations, a sequence of skills and formulas is presented, the packaging of the ideas substituting for their content. Technique then becomes wholly methodical, a set approach to a set list of technical problems involving all pianistic materials, and thus further away from the ideal of servicing the musical imagination.

Scales are not merely scales. There is no prototypical execution of a scale which can be applied in any circumstance; there is only a characteristic scale of special inflections appropriate to a singular circumstance. Deciphering and delineating this singularity, with the benefit of supple, responsive fingers, is the only subject worthy of consideration.

One does not wish to dismiss the legitimate preoccupation with technical facility—as long as it truly facilitates and serves the music. For technique is much more than a bill of particulars; it is the infinitely sensitive, fluent, and faithful means of rendering the composition's form and field. Technique is a retinue of beasts and battalions commandeered by the imagination for service to the Muse.

♩

Right notes and wrong notes can be counted. Perfection can be defined as the absence of mistakes, while brilliance and virtuosity are a function of measurable speed and decibels. The conventional world of technique has quantifiable features, providing a statistical basis for distinguishing the worth of various pianists. A society of consumers wants only the best, and the simplest, most demonstrable way of determining the best is to tally up the notes while applauding ever higher levels of speed and power. Poetic values are far too murky to permit such quantitative judgments.

These considerations are endemic to all societies of all ages. The very concept of performer embraces disciplines from the theater to the priesthood to basketball to music; implicit in these skills are the capacities of strength, stamina, projection, and consistency. Therefore, when we listen to pianists, we legitimately wish to appraise their technical command, but we are very lazy indeed if we confuse command with insight or virtuosity with art. Among the regrettable consequences of this laziness is the possibility that arresting and gifted artists are disqualified from performance careers because of some presumed flaw in their technical polish or consistency.

Lending itself to the same displacement of values is the phenomenon of recordings, the very symbol and emblem of quasi perfection. Rarely have so many blessings and so much mischief arisen from the same source.

♩

The quintessential marking in all Chopin piano scores targets the functional bass tone, controlling harmony and texture, which is frequently notated by the contradictory indications of *staccato* and pedal. The acoustical effect therefore should be both long and short in duration, presumably an invalid possibility by the laws of either/or and simultaneity.

But there is a confusion of circumstances in this account, for either/or applies only to a single source of activity or reference. There is, in this case, nothing to prevent the concurrence of an abrupt declamation which damps a portion of the sound at impact while permitting some degree of lingering sonority to remain. This is possible (and only possible) through skillful use of the pedal. Without control of its properties, the sound will be either anorexic or bloated. The pedal up, respecting the *staccato* sign, results in attrition; the pedal down, ignoring the *staccato*, produces glut.

The answer is readily available, but too rarely observed. The pedal goes down with the bass note, but releases only partly and immediately by a chosen fraction. The choice is left to the ear, the artistry, the acoustics of piano and chamber. The method requires an agile foot within the context of a sensibility that perceives artistic truth, by one essential perspective, as a function of the play between light and dark.

𝄢

The pedal is all. Not as it affects merely the notes, the dynamics, the timings, the textures, but all of these together in its role of gathering and siphoning, admitting and excluding the relevant sonorities. It is the benevolent dictator which decides all matters of execution or longevity. All individual notes are prey to its determinations, which advance the interests of the entire species alone.

The pedal does wondrous things. It can produce parallel tracks of opposite creatures, short and long, stable and flighty, silver and black, minnow and marlin, leaf and branch, atom and atmosphere, point and line, line and circle, all of which can be exercised, expanded, excised, and yet miraculously identified by its ever-vigilant magnanimity and discretion.

The pedal manipulates (peculiar oxymoron) the entire ensemble of resources, everything from solos to chorus. Insofar as the piece provides meanings and ambience—but more than that, a vocabulary and structure of sound, sound that is malleable, dynamic, and organized—then the pedal is the judge of first and last resort.

♭

In the G Minor Ballade of Chopin there is a passage marked *meno mosso*, beginning with the upbeat to bar 68 and the occasion of the second theme, which illustrates acutely the responsibilities and powers of the pedal. The figure in the right hand, other than in its opening and generating bar plus parallel example two bars later, consists entirely of single melody notes. The accompaniment in the left hand also employs nothing but single notes throughout the course of the fourteen-bar phrase, although two of its cadence tones are sustained briefly, creating a third overlapping voice which helps to close the phrase. Chopin's pedal marks are uncontroversial, and they coincide with the obvious harmonic changes.

The single notes of the left hand comprise a linear order which performs no less than five different tasks: (1) it provides a coherent meter and timing; (2) it forms the harmonic setting; (3) it establishes a contrapuntal line of independent melodic activity; (4) out of that line certain "motivic" notes delicately emerge to form a shadow third voice; (5) it engages in a dialogue with the right-hand melody that inevitably affects nuance, timing, and character.

The pedaling should conform to Chopin's stated intentions. Within that observance, however, there is a latitude which must be explored to accommodate the several tasks and purposes of the music. Only by the most sensitive shading of the pedal, exploiting the full range of its spectrum, can the vows, complexities, and liqueurs of this theme be aptly portrayed.

ọ

The right-hand melody of the aforementioned passage has, like any interesting and beautiful melody, unique characteristics of shape and emphasis. In this case, all of its patterns derive from the crucible of its first (and, by extension, third) bar. At the same time the motivic content of this bar is but a disarming transposition of a similar progression in the opening bar of the first and principal theme. In these two related progressions, harmony and melody merge at the outset to create a catalyst, both tense and fragrant, which invites the elaboration of their respective themes.

ọ

We call the melody the main voice. This is reasonable but deceiving. Nothing exists alone and out of context, and to the degree that the context is inadequately understood and delineated, the main voice or thesis loses its validity, loses profile and meaning.

For instance, the melody of the principal theme from Chopin's G Minor Ballade is notorious for its difficult prosody, complicated by the chordal textures derived by sustaining, according to Chopin's directions, the first three notes of its opening and recurrent motive. In the left-hand background, simple chords "harmlessly" fill out the rhythmic and harmonic functions. But these chords are not so harmless as they seem, and any conventional execution of them deflates the spirit of the whole.

Attached to these chords are three separate markings:

pedal for each repeated pair; slurs which group each pair; *staccato* marks added to each individual chord. The slur in conjunction with the *staccato* defines a throbbing, gently palpitating touch identified as *portato*. However, the usual smear of pedal afforded dissolves this poignant and idiomatic touch, producing a pseudo-tragic wash which despoils the character. A commonplace soap opera results, quite lacking in the special charm and insight of Chopin's notation. For the exquisite plaint of this theme is somehow compounded of part elegy, part *valse triste*, part reminiscence, and part lost innocence. Once again the pedal must mediate among the several touches, moods, and time zones.

But all beautiful melodies share essential and multiple properties. Not least is a psychological property which perhaps can best be described as representing a kind of spiritual alienation. For all melodies tend to remove themselves from the common ground of mundane experience, revealing their special spice and character by the usual devices of touch and *rubato*. Their expressive mission is to comment and extemporize on behalf of the caprices and solaces of personal will. If they are too passively integrated into the general mesh of sound, they sacrifice the prophetic, tender, and urgent qualities which mark them as independent of the collective reality.

Melodies are lovely creatures, narcissistic but noble. They must convey both the pain and the majesty of their isolation.

♩

The batting style of Lenny Dykstra, a superb outfielder for the Philadelphia Phillies, exemplifies and accentuates an ideal of coordination pertinent to all fields of performance. His style is especially instructive for pianists, bound to their benches and carrying the entire burden of music on their backs.

Dykstra is short and stocky in physical stature, and must use all the resources of his body to generate motion and power. He does this with a vengeance, quite literally, for he has a very aggressive, cheeky, tobacco-chewing stance that is geared to commit everything to his swing, body and soul. From the moment he steps into the batter's box, all his muscles and tendons begin to flex in rippling, circular sequence. From his toes to his twitching neck muscles, there is a constant, thrashing dance that revs up the juices and prepares for the one, flailing gesture. He uncoils like a whirling scythe, every ounce and limb contributing to the vortex of motion.

Pianists, whether demonstrative or sedate in their gestures, must still use all their resources, physical and spiritual. The gestures are abbreviated but no less active or malleable. No part of the body is sequestered, inert, dead. The desired character of the sound imposes its diagram and schedule, to which the body responds. All is weightless. Because the coordination is complete and universal, everything may soar. The tone soars because the mass has become liquid and the liquid has become air—or lighter than air. Spirit, both the spirit of conviction and the spirit of equilibrium, transmutes the mass.

Caution: the sanctity and sanity of the fingertips, ultimate agents, must be eternally protected.

THE TRANSFER

When choosing a student in piano, if that privilege be available, determine the level of mechanical facility, expressive range, and general intellectual tone. For if a young person cannot think, cannot feel, cannot concentrate, cannot run up and down the keyboard with some clarity and control, then playing the piano becomes an impossible task. These are the criteria, but they may be reduced to one: the parents. For without the love and support from mother or father or both, all the various gifts will prove inadequate and will wither.

ò

Brilliant students have brilliant parents, of the kind that shine forth in their devotion. Something different from vague hopes or strident ambition is involved. It is, rather, devotion to a kind of aesthetic and spiritual ideal which may be nameless, inchoate, even beyond the family experience or articulation. But it is passionately felt and communicated. More than a dream of glory, it comes closer to some conception of a paradise in which beauty and justice are permanently bound and enshrined. For these parents the leap of faith is rooted and pervasive. Heaven exists, is enchanted, and will be known through the diligence and sounds of their children.

ò

Such parents come in all temperaments and levels of sophistication. They can be crude, mute, or meddlesome. They can be deferential, enlightened, or gracious. They can be quietly persuasive or adamantly demanding. They can be chronically angry or sweetly suffering. They can be gentle, furious, or stoic, while dividing the carrot and stick between them. They can be positive reinforcers or negative scolds. But, finally, this is only a matter of style. Conceding that some styles are nicer than others, in the end one common conviction prevails. Hard work and noble deeds will make the other-world attainable to those sufficiently dedicated.

ò

If we are talking about music, it cannot be the illusion of prosperity which motivates these parents. So unpromising a profession cannot sustain such fictions. Even deluded parents know this, know the statistics, know the futility. Of course they may be seduced by certain myths, and will give lip service to these fairy tales as a means of persuasion.

But they know the odds, and they are not stupid. No, it is not the lust for success which burns inside them. It is a far more mystical light, rare and unexpected in so materialistic a culture. It is a dream of some Shangri-la which is timeless and benevolent. It is a vision of kindness and grace, made manifest through their child.

$$\diamond$$

Everybody says that we need better schools and education, an unexceptionable view. And so there will be competency tests for teachers, comprehensive educational standards, and the dismantling of tenure and seniority guidelines. In the face of academic mediocrity, society vents its wrath on the immediate target—and ignores the real culprit. Indeed, many of today's youth may be craven, uncouth, inarticulate, and greedy, while they tend to blame everybody else for their own failures of discipline and nerve. In other words, they are precise clones—and victims—of society. It is not better teachers but better mirrors that we need.

$$\diamond$$

If it were simply a matter of hiring better teachers, then the advice of the paleontologist Stephen Jay Gould would be irrefutable. Simply double their salaries, and the best and brightest would flock to this beleaguered profession. After all, Plato, among others, has observed that a nation will prosper to the degree that it honors its teachers. While certain historical examples might dispute the validity of this claim, it is yet reasonable to assume that honored and prosperous teachers would exert a proportionately greater influence over indifferent and recalcitrant youth. It may be a shocking hypothesis, but imagine the consequences if the history teacher were better known and paid than the football coach.

𝄞

In the unlikely event that teachers were more highly respected and compensated, it would represent more symptom than cause of educational progress. For the teacher is but the third layer of contact among the child's mentors. Parents and society are the essential crucibles, and only in extraordinary cases can good teaching overcome the effects of inadequacy in the primary agents. But for the musically precocious, above all, it is the parents who set the course, who form the vision and mold the destiny. It is only the parents who can contravene the social norms and pressures, who can serenade the child into that mythical kingdom of duty and song, of knights and minstrels, wherein the child, by solitary discipline, may secure the grail of blessed sound.

𝄞

Then it is up to the teacher to perpetuate the myth, to extend the romance, to provide the characters and the tools, the pragmatic suggestions, the distant concepts and exotic landscapes, the Amazons and heroes, the iridescent creatures, plumes, and stars, the stories of war, siege, and resistance, of courage and tenacity, of fighting with meager means, of exploiting the gods, the seasons, and the slow creep of time. The teacher is the guide who lives by principle alone, who is indifferent to fashion, who serves only his masters and the creations around him, whether man-made or god-made, and whatever is venturesome, proportioned, and inspired. He is a storyteller, but he tells the story to reveal the facts, finding the facts more astonishing and fantastical than the theories and embellishments often added to explain or adorn them.

𝄞

But it is not all sugar and spice. The teacher of the individual piano student, as the one in charge of the classroom, must make the case for work, routine, and concentration. The pupil becomes engaged, intrigued, captivated, until the I and Thou, subject and fact, achieve new levels of recognition and detail. Unexpected depths of personal feeling begin to surface while the musical score reveals surprising twists and turns. The progress occurs on both fronts. The individual soul becomes aware of its special resources, of its gift for imaginative assessments and sympathies. Similarly the object under study changes, sharpens, gains in intimacy and range, becomes ever more familiar and perplexing. The conditions for discovery are quiet, peace, boundaries, and intense fascination. For an idea which is acknowledged but unfelt is like a winning lottery ticket uncashed.

ạ̊

Given the clutter of contemporary life and the saturation of events, people, and media, the advice of Artur Schnabel to "practice in tranquillity" might seem welcome to most. But the youthful mind has been so fragmented and truncated by the collision of images and dissociation of meanings that the fundamental sequences of both time and logic have largely been shattered. For most youths (and their elders) it is very difficult to break through the addictive cycles of interruption and disintegration. Only the most determined efforts of those anointed parents and surrogate teachers will steer some children free from the cultural traffic jams. Given the odds, no more heroic task can be conceived.

ạ̊

Albert Einstein once said that often the best teacher is a stupid pedant. In this connection one recalls that Beethoven, a student of Haydn but wary of his teacher's propensity for anecdotes and general bonhomie, departed for the more

conservative master, Johann Georg Albrechtsberger, to receive instruction in strict counterpoint. Moral: There is no
meaningful freedom without form, no language without
syntax, no art without structure.

The young child's hand at the piano is usually formless, however sympathetic to the musical flow. The concept
of the "correct" hand position is nonetheless wholly chi-
merical. But the hand, as an articulate agent of musical
meanings and distinctions, must be cultivated. It must be
shaped, nurtured, and honored in its role as the embodiment of touch and expression, of phrasing and diction. But
only after it is formed can it be re-formed to fulfill the
needs of suppleness, power, and that depth of sonority necessary to liberate the extremes of color and feeling.

𝒬

A senior musician of highest reputation once marked
down a student of mine in a competitive situation by the
curt appraisal "unmusical." This student is now an active
concert pianist with a burgeoning career. His crime was a
failure to offer that agreeable and wholesome exterior
through which the music "swings and sways," thereby expressing the values of motherhood, apple pie, and that
tender resignation sure to please the listener. For what we
want in our performers is a sense and spirit in which they
accept their lot as entertainers and as guardians of cultural
conventions.

Other students of mine, also less attractive on the musicality scale, may yet possess remarkable gifts of mind,
passion, and execution. For the moment the geniality quotient eludes them, either out of inhibition or disinterest.
Of course, the smooth contours of melodies and phrases are
a subject for legitimate inquiry, but as a category of expression this particular facility is but one pearl among the

many treasures of conviction and fire which may beat within.

♀

When we characterize a student as "unmusical," it may indicate a failure of our own imagination. Some students, by rounding off their phrases, their appearances, their repertoires (to a carefully chosen ration), may please by a spurious wholesomeness which is but the measure of modest gifts nicely stitched together. Easily overlooked and rarely acknowledged in the audition/competition process are the two attributes which are vital to genuine talent.

The first is productivity, the capacity to learn, ingest, and digest the quantity of material necessary to know the literature and to participate in the profession. The range and wisdom of the literature will be known only through contact with a great variety of individual pieces, which are more important to teaching than the teacher.

The second desirable trait is the need for a special characteristic to emerge from the general mix of the student's skills. If all the skills are homogeneously blended ("musical"), it is unlikely that the student will develop the requisite force of personality. Some specific feature of technique, temperament, or intellect must be available, in the same sense that the great tennis player possesses at least one "killer" stroke or gift. The attribute "musical" often betrays the absence of such a gift.

♀

Making judgments that would arbitrarily distinguish "musical" from "unmusical" children is parallel to the educational system in certain countries which determines, at some threshold age, whether a youth is better suited for professional or vocational training. In both cases, the judgments are premature and cavalier.

No child, no person is fundamentally unmusical, except to the degree that he has been broken, stifled, beaten, bored, or simply worn out by despair or violence—for which wounds music may be the best therapy. Rilke called it "all the unlived lines of our faces," when describing the fatigue and repression written into our countenance, our soul. Surely common sense as well as anthropological evidence documents the universal need to pray, to hope, and to lament or carouse through song.

♩

To put it bluntly (with a blush toward Elgar), this studio does not well tolerate the pap and circumventions of the youthful environment. Too many seedy activities translate into decadent minds and spirits. Our operative principles are work, ideals, and thoroughness. To make the mind grow and the soul prosper requires concentration, plus a profound sympathy for all the grand constructs of nature and man. When we discuss the structure of music, for instance, we do not exclude such metaphors as the structure of a butterfly's wing, from whose intricate tracings we may conjure up the buttresses, gables, and ribbing of a Gothic cathedral.

The first word we learn is *No*. No to extraneous, debilitating habits and activities which rob the musician of his most precious currency, time. No to all the smothering gruel and pastiche of incongruencies which deflect the processes of cognition and sequential thought. No to those peer blandishments which dilute individuality.

Yes to reading, to kindness, to productivity, to inquiry and discussion, to a decent respect for the affairs of mankind and the wonders of nature.

♩

No is the prelude to the first act. The first act dwells upon a single theme, which is the premise of the entire play and all the plays and redemptions that follow. This theme revolves around a single word and concept, its Spartan message (but with vast retinue) the most routine thought in the entire language, routine itself.

Without a pattern and consistency of work, there is no joy in Mudville. We strike out, doomed to repeat the same futile and aimless gestures. The pattern need not be "routine": some work better by day, some by night; some, for practical reasons, stuff the bulk of their work into weekdays or weekends; some produce on a curve of their own devising; whatever, the routine must have a pattern, must replicate itself, must be consistent. The ideal routine is daily work.

Work should challenge the mind, the senses, the spirit —and be agreeable. The main thing is to persuade your student to feel genuinely and legitimately content after a good day's work. Progress is gratifying, success is a great stimulus, but work itself must be inherently satisfying, and should supersede material rewards as the primary source of pleasure.

Therefore, music must always be celebrated as a puzzle of infinite charm, and as the road to self-awareness and self-esteem. Which is but a reasonable description of its intrinsic and therapeutic values.

♭

One is interested in how students think, their qualities of perception, their ability to make distinctions, associations, choices—the dictionary definitions of intellect, imagination, and intelligence.

Too few of them can string the words together to form an intelligible sentence. This may not be a fatal flaw. For some, however, it could mark the stunting of cognitive skills, a natural reaction to an inchoate environment bursting with wisecracks and distractions. For these children a profound appeal to basic standards of sense and justice is prerequisite to restoring faith in distinctions of value. For they must believe that one thing is more important than another, and then worth saying. The urgency and discrimination of their music-making is vitally related.

But for a few who are chronic mumblers and mutterers, the problem may be different. This small sect fixates on the world of spirit and symbols, though deficient in the terms of its description. Their muttering is a sign of adoration for nameless saints. Their dismembered syntax is a way of groping for distant fields.

ρ

Thinking at the piano comes in several varieties. First there is the bare-bones blueprint, organizational thinking which subdivides the material on a local, passage-by-passage basis. Recognition of the groupings, motivic and rhythmic, which form the construction blocks of the passage should precede the hand's attempt to assimilate the material. Deciphering and delimiting these patterns is essential to technical control and general fluency. (I am forever recommending puzzle books and Sherlock Holmes adventures to my students as primers for deducing and sorting the evidence.)

Then there is the kind of structural thinking which explores larger sections for their formal and harmonic relationships, not least by the tendencies to repeat, vary, or develop their content. The fundamental law of musical memory (and form) is determined by identifying what is the same, what is different, and by how much.

Finally, there is the thinking which gives meaning to the notes. On this level no student is fully equipped, and many are poorly endowed. Which is not their fault, but the fault of what has been given to them, mindscape and landscape.

♀

I have struggled to offer my students some token of those works of art and nature which conceivably form the resonant choir of meanings and allusions for individual pieces. Sometimes one appeals to the native habitat of both student and work, so that for a Russian pupil the image of Dr. Zhivago's Lara seemed useful to evoking a forlorn idealism in the second theme of the first movement of Rachmaninoff's Third Piano Concerto. But we all employ such kinds of references in a spirit of equal mischief and urgency. Sometimes these props are playful and irreverent; other times they are a desperate reach to encourage a special, idiomatic sound.

But on certain occasions, the intellectual and imaginative deficiencies require more formal and comprehensive measures. Thus my teacher taught me the subtleties and ironies of chess. In exchange I tried to instruct him in the rules of baseball, until one day he stumped me by pointing out that it would be a much easier game if the pitcher and the batter were on the same team.

♀

I have asked one student to prepare a short discourse on the subject of chiaroscuro in painting, another to buy some plants and write an essay on the cycle of their growth, another to work up a list of twenty-five similes for the image of a samovar. Nothing heavy or pursued in any demanding way, but simply exercises for the mind to be continued indefinitely.

Some flexibility, some freedom, some poetry of thought make for bridges to the music, give it dimension and the aura of noble deeds. For many youths, piano playing has been relegated to a show of filial respect and gymnastic skills. One wants to remind them, persistently, that making music is an artistic venture, and that they are artists-in-the-making.

One also wants to remind them that the context of music is varied and profound. If their fantasy is to be awakened —so that their sounds may be incisive or ravishing—then the menagerie of saints and dragons must be faithfully recalled.

♭

The overabundance of gifted students has exacerbated a problem of cultural dictates and personal conscience. Individual teachers must pause before guiding their talented pupils into a society which has little sustaining need for them. Piano playing is perhaps the most demanding discipline and, other than the spasmodically brief careers of gymnasts and figure skaters, requires the most work over the long run. It is difficult work; it is lonely, repetitious, frustrating, and the rewards are ephemeral. The occasional gold star, the murmurs of approval for an appearance on the annual recital, the heartfelt but halting pride of the parents—this can be a meager diet without the love for music.

But the students play away, riding on a thread of habit and hope. And their souls, in some sporadic and awkward way, expand. They detect the potential for genuine personal identity, as distinct from communal fashions and peer submersion. The increasing complexity and challenge of the pieces they work on advance new and more radical, or old and more traditional, visions of human capacity. They are thus incipient artists, trafficking in noble ideas and utopian schemes for improving the lot of mankind.

Let them study the piano. Society needs them.

♩

I am blessed with remarkable students; thus rarely do I face the crisis of advising them whether to go on with their piano studies or to try something else. But some of them attend Harvard and have bright, snappy minds for a variety of subjects. Should they follow the path of winning a Nobel Prize in physics, or should they become good and under-loved pianists hustling for students in the suburbs? Of course there are also jobs in settlement schools, community colleges, and junior colleges which, with luck, could be the prelude to a position at a university. Or one or two of them might win a fair-sized competition, making them more desirable candidates for the meager spoils system. And yet, how many of them can really develop a substantial career as a performing pianist, their dearest and unsecret wish? Why not sober up the whole lot of them, to make their futures more manageable, more comfortable?

A long time ago my teacher stared out the window of his apartment at the garbage truck sweeping the street below. His dear friend commented on the injustice of social rewards by pointing out that the driver of the truck probably earned more money than did the remarkable musician standing next to him. "Perhaps," replied my teacher, "but somehow I'd rather play the piano."

♩

Does not the soul have a belly too? And so we are likely to spend our lives feeding basic instincts, or the instincts vulnerable to current props and scams. They say hamburgers are no good for you, but they're tasty and you have to eat. I would mention a lot of other things that are no good for you, things that are pleasing, that are pretty, that are sweet and filling and fill the belly and habits of both mind and soul. It is nice to earn a good living; it is nice to have

money and fine things; it is nice to have spare time and
spare cash to go to the opera. But it is also nice to make
music and to know oneself, to know one's soul, its roots
and branches, to be fulfilled if not filled up.

When I am asked by students, mine or not, talented or
not, whether to continue on in music, I do not hesitate.
Perhaps that is unconscionable, not hesitating, but how can
I reject the instinct to self-awareness, to prowl around the
bittersweet of consciousness, to take those gingerly steps to
recognition of self or that selflessness which is not dependent but free? And one always has a firm guide, the musical
scores which could not survive unless crafted by reason and
ethics. It is not the teacher who teaches the student; it is
the teacher who guides the student to the scores which
teach—if the teacher knows the score.

𝄐

The goal for each student is always the same—independence. And the goal for every teacher should be the
cultivation of the student's independence.

There are two primary constituents of independence: musical judgment and personal identity. As for judgment,
the essential strategy is to provide the means for making
reasoned choices on a variety of levels. The teacher must
explain why alternative solutions to problems of interpretation are not only plausible but defensible. Given the surfeit of notational evidence, which is then qualified by
stylistic idioms, intrinsically there are endless gradations,
relationships, voicings to be determined. And of course each
individual voice can be scanned according to different
schemes of emphasis and shaping. The plethora of choices
involved should be investigated, enjoyed, and idealized as
sample of music's boundless freedom.

As for the personal identity of the student, particular

care should be given to the repertoire assigned. The pieces suggested should in some way mirror the inner nature of the student, but with provision for some works contrary to that nature to encourage new growth. True artists identify themselves by their choice of programs. Give a student the same conventional pieces his colleagues play, and in the end you will have an ordinary student playing in a conventional way.

$\natural$

The painter Fernand Léger is reported to have said that he would not trust a student who, at some point, did not tell his teacher to go to hell. While I have been unable to prompt such active rebellion, this message becomes painfully clear, by inversion, when a student unconsciously copies my playing—for the effect is ghastly. For a teacher, the student's independence is far more flattering than imitation.

All students, however immature, have an identifiable sound, or "voice," which must be recognized and salvaged. Sometimes this quality is in such an embryonic stage as to be nearly undetectable. All the more need then to rescue its core, give it flesh and wings, and mark the center of a burgeoning personality.

This recognition warrants consistent affirmation of the vulnerable core. And if the individual approach of the student does not conform to stylistic conventions of the day, not to worry, for standards change all the time and often for the worse. As the great paintings and frescoes of the past have survived all calamities of weathering, corrosion, and cleaning—until nobody knows what the originals looked like—so great music survives the normal pendulum of interpretive approaches plus a good deal of other mischief or purification. These variations of sound and style seem an almost necessary homage to confirm the limitless implications of the music. Correspondingly, our students should be invited to discover their own natures by exploring the full range of these implications.

♮

The primary function of the teacher is to teach vocabulary, the vocabulary of sound, of diction, of feeling. When a writer such as Ernest Hemingway confines himself to a spare, unvarnished prose, or when a poet such as Constantine Cavafy intentionally eschews metaphor, they are making deliberate choices within a range of infinite possibilities. That their words are vivid, searing, uncompromising is in some measure the result of the tension between their choices and the pile of unused choices they disdain. (André Gide observes that what the writer *doesn't* say is of more importance than what he does say.)

Provide the students with several possibilities of sound and statement, and then let them choose. Play back for them, by person or machine, the choices or non-choices they make, and then inquire if these are intended or accidental. Demonstrate the passage with models of different inflections and colors so as to make them potential components of future decisions. Let the students enjoy the tangle and clutter of experiment, the variety of paths which lead to the ring of truth. Let them experience the innumerable gradations and dialects of sound as essential preliminaries to their delimiting choices. Thus train the ear, which must become the author of their fate and, one is always reminded, of the fate of the composition.

♮

An exceptionally talented and serious student of my wife's never tires of asking fundamental questions about music and all other related and unrelated matters. Each answer provokes two new questions, and the more she knows the more unhappy she is. She insists upon knowing not only what she should think, do, and choose, but why it is necessary and right. She is the ideal student.

In her genes there is a spirit which demands not only clear distinctions between right and wrong but, above all, the rationale for making these distinctions. What is as yet unclear to her are the necessarily different criteria applicable to separate categories of values.

If one talks about practical life or legal principles, then common sense and precedent will identify concrete alternatives of good and bad, of acceptable and unacceptable. Yes, you should brush your teeth three times a day, and no, you should not drive while drunk. When it comes to moral life, the distinctions become blurred. Yes, charity is the noblest impulse of man toward others; yes, charity begins at home.

When we discuss aesthetic considerations, wherein beauty and truth reside in both mortal combat and embrace, the variables of right and wrong are forever in a state of dynamic tension. Perhaps this is why Marcel Duchamp said, "There are no answers, because there are no questions." Other, perhaps, than the one wondrous question, How is this universe possible? And then, How can one describe it?

ê

The most telling comment I have encountered on the dilemma of teaching is contained in the preface to Arnold Schoenberg's text on harmony. He points out the obvious fact (but of such sobering impact it is generally repressed) that most teachers teach the student what they know, while few teachers teach the student what the student doesn't know.

Think of it. Do we not usually assign our most familiar and favorite pieces to our pupils? Do we not favor styles of interpretation reflecting our own backgrounds and traditions? Do we not invoke methods of technical discipline reflecting the training and habits of our own hands? Do we not recommend the reading material we know best and take comfort in? Do we not assume that our students, though of diverse nature and talent, emerge from a homogenous environment which bestows upon them similar predispositions? Do we not, therefore, and out of habit itself, suggest and repeat the same formulas of development, of musical style, of physical posture, of technique, philosophy, repertoire, fingering, and of everything else which accommodates our own schemes and images of achievement, but which may not oblige the needs of individual students, their strengths, weaknesses, and ideals?

ọ

Curriculum requirements for each student should be differentiated according to individual needs and goals. If one student requires more counterpoint and the other more solfège, why feed the same portions to disproportionate needs? Why not tailor a curriculum which could respond to and compensate for personal strengths and weaknesses?

Probably for the practical and defensible reason that class loads would fluctuate unpredictably, as would faculty contracts and responsibilities. The solution would involve clever planning, flexibility, and the likelihood that imbalances in the student profiles would cancel out, thus precluding massive shifts to or from a given subject. Or if some such shift became pronounced, it would provide a reasonable index for rearranging the curriculum and faculty roster accordingly.

Mandatory requirements should be reduced in general.

Of course, a certain standard of musicianship must be upheld, but it is arbitrary and mechanical for a school to ignore the considerable variations of skills and deficiencies in each student's portfolio. To be fluent in one subject and ignorant in another makes for a shaky preparation for the future; such disparities cannot be addressed by a simple uniform standard. Conversely, students should have the option of exploring that variety of subjects, however specialized, which may lead them to their own private destiny. We are in the business of training artists, not audiences.

♭

The persistent quandary of a conservatory education issues from the difficulty of integrating applied and theoretical studies. Typically there is minimal feedback between the student's work in the areas of harmony, analysis, even music literature, and his specialized approach to performance. The jugular vein is severed, for the distinctive jargons of theory do not easily translate to pragmatic instrumental problems, while the zones of private interpretation tend to simmer in their own mystical or mundane juices. The separation tends to be absolute; the student makes little effort to relate the banks of information.

Therefore, and for similar reasons which flow from the chronic pique between performers and musicologists, we have bushels of talented pianists who may achieve a modicum of success, but who merely embellish without contributing to the culture. The special insights and wisdom which can come only from understanding the musical language, its signs, structures, precedents, and history are innocently subsumed into the tender platitudes of pianistic touch and gesture, or, worse, betrayed by the vanities of bravura indulgence. The issues of musicianship are considered academic. Theory and piano are as far removed as are

French and chemistry. Analysis is for and about fossils; performance is a form of corruption. Thus materializes the danger of the unwitting and artificial separation of mutually essential perspectives.

ò

The development of a course which could combine the perspectives of several disciplines is not unrealistic, other than the problem of breaking through the logjam of institutional habit. In fact, such a course could conceivably become the symbol of an approach integrating all information relevant to any work of music. It is really quite simple: over the semester one or two pieces would be comprehensively discussed by members of the theory, performance, history, and humanities departments in symposium style. All aspects, semantics, precedents, and visions of the work could then coalesce into some fabric of understanding. The student would discern, finally, both the genealogy and the uniqueness of the compositional process, as well as the salient correspondences between form and meaning.

The exceptional students I am fortunate to work with present a different set of problems from those in the average class. For one thing, their technical facility and standard of preparation are on such a high level as to allow us to concentrate on matters of interpretation, minimizing the time spent on shoptalk and practical considerations. On the other hand, each of them has earned the right to anticipate a concert career. This means that we must aim not only for the highest standard of performance but also for that performance which avows the uniqueness of both piece and player. There is a proud motto in our studio: Perfection is not the goal but the point of departure.

I engage in an active, interventionist sort of teaching, not at all sitting back and philosophizing about life and music. We do plenty of that on the telephone, but during the lesson it is intense business, constant demonstration, cries of alarm and approval. Notes may be missed but not casually flubbed. Phrases may be askew but not aimlessly drifting. Sonorities may be brazen but not barren. The player has to say something, with verve and style. Every note counts and is a candidate for the day of judgment.

As they play through their pieces, I hover to the side, braying, pleading, dancing to the musical flow, but also guiding the reluctant finger to the specific and desired dynamic. For the detail and the whole must couple; their fates are inextricably bound.

ò

My teacher, Edward Steuermann, with whom I studied for some fifteen years, taught me music. Of course he also taught me how to play the piano, but the piano was an instrument for making music. The piano had its own canon and lore, its rare aphrodisiacs of sound, trembling, and power, its wicked problems of inflection and execution, and its special prowess for distinguishing several voices. The piano was enigmatic and magical, a fantastic toy and invention, a singular force which could slay all demons and cherish all angels, a space vehicle, a binding symbol, omnipotent, charming, infinite.

Such was the piano. But it was there for making music, and you learned it well to make better music. In my lifetime great pianists have abounded; some have used music to play the piano, and a few have used the piano to make music.

Thus he tried to train me, and so he taught me harmony, counterpoint, and composition, plus a few other incidentals like chess, and how to be responsible and reasonable. It was not just the piano; it was music that he tried to plant in my bratty head, being a kid of eleven when I had my first lesson with him.

ℓ

My teacher also taught me manners and to respect the rights of others. Once, when in the middle of a late lesson at his studio, I flipped on the piano lamp as twilight approached. Rather sharply he switched it off. I felt flushed with embarrassment, yet instantly recognized that this was not a show of stinginess but a lesson in propriety. First ask when it isn't yours. On another occasion he introduced me to his longtime student, an elegant woman who joined us in a cab as we went off to the movies. Like many adolescents, I gave the usual inarticulate grunt of greetings. No, no, he protested; when you meet a lady you must always say, *"Enchanté!"* As was almost always the case, he did not embarrass me by my ignorance. The charm and twinkle of his eye encouraged the pleasures of decent manners and discourse. Life and music were full of sweet surprises and agreeable detours. The role and the privilege of being a musician implied a life without gloom, without pedantry.

I learned from him, as best as I could, decency, tolerance, courage, and the indifference of appearances. Growing up in a rather plastic culture, I was grateful to have it affirmed that a man's heart was more important than his bankroll.

ℓ

Mr. Steuermann was not keen on celebrities, was even rather suspicious of them. The whole pattern of his life was based upon a devotion to music—to new music and its sobering, prophetic message, to old music as a source of wisdom and courage, but not at all to the music of self-indulgence and career addiction. This had nothing to do with any aversion to light or charming or tuneful music, for he knew by heart the operettas by Franz Lehár and could even rattle off a few Jerome Kern tunes. He appreciated beautiful melodies for their own sake, lamenting once that the trouble with Rachmaninoff was that you could never get the "damn" tunes out of your head.

But as a pupil of Busoni and Schoenberg, two of the noblest, most idealistic of musicians, he had little patience with musical operators, charlatans, and peacocks. Fame, of which he had a considerable amount, though more in Europe than in America, where he had emigrated in the 1930s, was quite incidental, and in some way a sign of compromise with fashion.

Since he was not in the habit of cultivating the celebrities of the day, his students were surprised to find a sealed recording by Arthur Rubinstein of the Beethoven *Appassionata* on his coffee table. Six weeks later it was still there, still sealed. "Why haven't you heard it?" somebody asked. With his characteristic mixture of levity and self-mockery, he replied, "Because I'm afraid I might like it."

Ωo

Perhaps it is because of an unconscious lust for monarchy, or for the pecking order of the totem pole, or for those dominant deities or males who secure the territory, or for the serenity that issues from a fixed hierarchy—whichever, we are happiest when the problem of choice is blissfully removed. We love to determine who is number one, who is queen for a day, who is in or out, at the top or bottom of the barrel, ranked highest on the computer or fading fast—and in musical performance, who offers the greatest satisfaction, thrill, and claim to precedence.

The question of which athlete puts the shot farthest can easily be resolved by measuring the distance of the throw. The matter of ranking tennis players is more nebulous despite the computer, for conditions, entry lists, and the luck of the draw fluctuate so widely. In the realm of art, beyond a certain threshold of competence and conviction, it is futile and infantile to assert priority, but the only people who resist this lust are the artists themselves.

Thus when a student asked Mr. Steuermann whether he preferred the Clifford Curzon or Rudolf Serkin interpretation of the Brahms D Minor Piano Concerto, my teacher replied gruffly, "How the hell would I know? I have enough trouble figuring out how the music goes myself."

$♩$

A UCLA study suggests that people who own pets visit the doctor sixteen percent less often than people who do not own pets. The implications of this study are modest indeed, yet deserving of some comment.

Familiarity with nonhuman beings allows students to understand the life cycle in a more detached, unthreatening way. As well, the instinct for taking care, for responsibility itself, would be better nurtured in our young if they were squire to pets or wildlife. As for incipient artists, contact with animals of remarkable and lithe grace illuminates capacities which explore the spectrum of natural forms and energies, of coordinated gestures which inspire the mind's gift for pattern and invention. (I think of the composer Stefan Wolpe, describing his music by reference to the swirling, darting trajectories of fish he had observed at the aquarium.)

When one is teaching the motions and maneuvers which negotiate the keyboard, the natural agility of animals provides revealing example and stimulus. Even the dreaded snake may offer testimony of the note-by-note crawling necessary to manage a smooth *legato*. In gliding along the keys, the full apparatus of finger, hand, arm, and torso is channeled into the linear design. Our gross weight slips through the needle eye of the line.

ϙ

When I think about the ideal of teaching, I do not have very far to turn. I think about what my wife has accomplished, vivid both to the ear and in the results and awards her students have earned.

Most teachers concentrate on one perspective or another. They teach the interpretation, or the style, or the technique, or the hand position, or the body posture, breathing, psychology of performance, structure, Schenker, beautiful tone, imagery, discipline, what to wear for different occasions—or various combinations thereof. My wife teaches all of the above and more. The more is responsibility, which is the basis of pride, which is the basis of a performance ethic. The students are responsible for presenting themselves presentably. If they squirm and shirk their way out of the agreed assignment, they will not be branded with a scarlet letter, but their consciences will labor and twitch. Better their minds should labor, they soon find out.

Otherwise she is like a shepherd, circling round the flock of ambling habits. Each stray note, each faulty and uninspired execution is identified, invigorated, and brought into the fold. The chain is as strong as the weakest link, and my wife runs a pretty good chain gang. But she does it with an interest and love so palpable that her students have no choice but to flourish.

ϙ

When a certain student lamented his inadequate phrasing to Mr. Steuermann, my teacher politely replied, "Why don't you see a *phraseur?*"

The moral of this story is quite simple. In piano playing, everything is related and nothing can forcibly be dragged out of context. The phrasing may be isolated as a symptom or branch of the organism, but repairing it involves many coordinated factors. Even if only a single line is indicated in the score, harmonic implications, metric matters, dramatic strategies are all active players. Whether few or many notes, all the musical and imaginative parameters are present and operative. It is this feeling for the entire organism, this mutual dependence of all the compositional elements participating in a comprehensive vision of the work, which distinguishes the effective and enlightened performance.

What distinguishes the effective and enlightened teacher is that resourcefulness which addresses all the issues and their ultimate coordination. What distinguishes my wife's teaching is just such a resourcefulness and one which is impervious to fatigue or indifference. She is a far-ranging hawk who will scratch with one claw and offer tasty morsels with the other. Her eyes are her ears, and they do not miss any scrap of sound or meaning.

♭

The solo piano repertoire affords the possibility of creating a self-sufficient world which has many subjects and landmarks to be acknowledged and cared for. The problem is in covering the full terrain, knowing every knoll and ridge of each given piece, every shape, color, and dimension destined for inclusion on the great map.

It is a difficult but deducible task. First, one gives identities and names to the musical events. These names have two faces, one bound by the laws of notation, the other boundless in the regions of character and expression. Then comes the always volatile task of gathering these events into a coherent stream. This is performance, a constantly improvising dynamic of compatible and incompatible ideas—living, breathing, restful, restless, happening, this one moment, inimitable, as though walking a tightrope strung between mountaintops, singing of sky and land while yet negotiating the wind currents.

Coordination: this is what the teacher must begin and end with. As I stand next to the student I feel dangerously like a puppeteer trying to guide him or her through the vortex of ideas and feelings. I console myself in the realization that eventually students will internalize this role and learn to master their own fate.

𝄐

I have all kinds of students in my rather small class: dynamos, aristocrats, pioneers, Sapphos, Apollonians, Newtonians, chameleons, melancholians, lynxes, and onyxes—in fact, one of each, that makes ten. Now let them figure out which is which. They all share one gift in common. They move. You put the needle on and out comes a performance.

Sometimes it is green, or grim, or gritty, but they move, they are malleable; and they have a soul which it is my job to welcome. Now the work begins. Play it through, dear chameleon, and we will muse on your blemishes and beauties. Good. More song, more text, more elegant, less neutral. Read this poem, look at that painting, distill your joy and sympathies into a few minutes of release, revelation, passion according to Saint Frédéric. Now, once more; let us go through it again.

This time I float nearby, ready to pounce. Every note must yield—flowers, grain, but not corn. I gather up strength, the vision of my teacher, trust in our mission. Listen! Your ears must guide this team of wild huskies, your fingers must steer the breathless, exhilarating course. Watch here, watch there, full-out, shhh, *sforzando!*, balance, *dolce* . . .

◊

There are two kinds of piano teachers: those who assign the pieces with which they are most familiar, and those who don't. Liszt, for instance, would generally refuse to hear any work which he considered a *"spécialité de la maison."* The bittersweets of intimacy made it too painful (or sacrilegious) to invite strangers to walk on such hallowed ground.

But all teachers are likely to recommend certain favorite composers and pieces deemed useful to the growing-up stages of their students. To promote discrimination of ear and execution, some teachers assign Bach; others start with Chopin as the ground of touch and control. For me, the exemplary guide and mind-opener is Haydn.

Haydn instructs in thinking: heart-thinking and brain-thinking. Haydn instructs in faith; Haydn instructs in skepticism. Haydn instructs in resolve and in resignation; in structure and strategy; in caprice and tenderness. Haydn instructs, above all, in that which is root, premise, and condition of all else: *composition*, or how the notes are put together, broken apart, reassembled, and transformed. Everything is up-front, exposed. Life is tragic, life is amusing; things come and go; one is at the center of the storm, and at the periphery.

For the notes are alive. They create and crumble right in front of our bloodied nose.

◊

Haydn provides a pedagogical example in one other respect, a lesson imperative to contemplate in this day of media glut, of the siren call of cheap fame, and of the triumph of notoriety over talent. In his writings Haydn reflected on the fortunate fact of his relative isolation at the Esterhazy estate, where he served as music man to the prince. For a crucial period of maturity and growth, he was thankful to be distant from Vienna, from the center of fashion and commerce, and thus allowed him to develop his own ideas, personality, and vision.

For a vivid endorsement of that individuality which must be protected, and which must flourish for the artist to survive, I quote from the notebooks of Gerard Manley Hopkins, who unsentimentally identifies the chief agent of artistic personality, the self.

> *Nothing else in nature comes near this unspeakable stress of pitch, distinctiveness, and selving, this selfbeing of my own. Nothing explains it or resembles it, except so far as this, that other men to themselves have the same feeling . . . Searching nature, I taste self but at one tankard, that of my own being. The development, refinement, condensation of nothing {else} shows any sign of being able to match this to me or give me another taste of it, a taste even resembling it . . . When I compare my self, my being-myself, with anything else whatever, all things alike, all in the same degree, rebuff me with blank unlikeness; so that my knowledge of it, which is so intense, is from itself alone, they in no way help me to understand it. And even those things with which I in some sort identify myself, as my country or family, and those things which I own and call mine, as my clothes and so on, all presuppose the stricter sense of self and me and mine and are from that derivative.*

Without that core of independence and self-awareness, a core protected from the winds of fashion, easy access, or intimidation, a person cannot make the profound and steely judgments which separate chaff from essence, and by which he may better apprehend the object, the other, as a source for study and admiration.

♭

The large cities of the world provide a treasure trove of culture and its artifacts, of concerts, theaters, museums, and libraries nurturing the forces of creation and appreciation. In some instances, however, they can also inhibit creation, as well as the imagination of minds young and old stretching back into time and ahead, needing sun, space, and solitude to pursue interior visions and their external models. In particular, when that city is the locus of the culture industry and all its appurtenances of success, market, and rat race, judgment is easily shriveled by the appeal to Mammon. And in particular, when that city is drowned in traffic, noise, garbage, derelicts, and dereliction, in foul displays and distortions of wealth and poverty, in hordes of homeless, in sunless streets dominated by monolithic buildings, in the concrete slabs and jackhammers that wring and wrench the earth of its green and grace, of the patterns and colors that feed inspiration and are the very blueprint and green print of art, then I would suggest that this may not be the right place for self, for growing up, for an independent perspective on the goods and griefs of life.

For such a place becomes parochial by its self-absorption, absorbing selves into its quest for a novelty strikingly unoriginal. In the home of deals and turnovers, only sensations survive, and their shelf life diminishes radically and exponentially. Parents of the world, consider well before sending your children to such a town. They may become members of an anonymous audience with shiftless, shifting standards. Send them to places with great cathedrals and vistas, and with parks that tolerate lovers and inspire a loving eye.

THE CONTEXT

There are two kinds of musicians: creationists and evolutionists. The former believe in the fixed identity of each piece in the literature, according to the established characteristics of the given composer and era. These are the Platonists. The Aristotelians (and Zen Buddhists) have no such divine map. The work of art, though bound by its genetic markings and indelible fingerprints, is boundless in the infinite elaborations of its destiny, and therefore in the range of its interpretations.

◊

Shakespeare esteems the rose to the canker-bloom, on the grounds that its special fragrance affords an additional dimension to the visible beauty they both share. The distinguishing threshold of the lasting work of art, beyond the essential quality of craft and feeling, resides in the degrees of ambiguity, of multiple meanings available to its tangible and intangible evidence.

◊

If a work of art can be solved or even comprehended, then it is of minor value. When people hear "satisfying" performances of great pieces, they are usually responding to shared prejudices, which feature the prevailing ethic to the detriment of the creative labyrinth. Thus the "received idea," joint property of both experts and public, will almost always triumph over the discourse of thesis and contradiction intrinsic to profound and eventful works.

◊

In contemporary performance practice, the natural tension between the antithetical poles of unity and variety has been gravely skewed in behalf of the former. There are many reasons for this, such as the general suspicion of rhetoric, the catatonic submission to the urtext mentality, and the effect of proliferating recordings, which often are more the product of producer than performer. But chief villain is the saturation of incongruous stimuli which assault our senses from every quarter of the cultural environment, leaving us defenseless and prey to simple, monolithic solutions.

◊

Thus Beethoven becomes the prince of German idealism, noble, pure, and grandiose. But Beethoven the eccentric, the radical, the adventurer is too dangerous, too heady and intoxicating for our pious complacency as distilled from a therapeutic escapism. We prefer the slogans that simplify, that purge.

ℓ

Curiously Bach, the most ecclesiastically rooted composer in our pantheon, has invited the widest and freest range of interpretations as legitimized by general practice. But Chopin, the most vulnerable surveyor of the fantasy world, must be played with "classical" rectitude (i.e., with a statically homophonic texture and diction), or the experts will howl. Our preoccupation with the morbid makes us recoil from a subject matter we falsely construe as morbid. We clean it up and banish the ghosts.

ℓ

The polyphony of Bach is represented by a network of independent lines which contrast and combine. The polyphony of Chopin expresses itself as an aggregate of diverse textures, mixing durations, colors, and registers in an endless colloquy which disperses and reassembles the components of sound. Of all Chopin notations, the staccato bass note with pedal affixed remains the paradigm, a paradox distilled to a truth.

ℓ

The work of art inevitably spills over its chronological and idiomatic boundaries. Chopin is the disciple of Bach and Mozart, and as well the forerunner of Scriabin. Any performance of Chopin which amputates these and other antennae to past and future must lie by omission, must retreat toward a banal platitude.

ℓ

The implications of a work of art do not merely comprise its surrounding penumbra. A reality without possibilities is but a hollow reflex. Any juxtaposition of two notes in their respective contexts becomes a source of aesthetic and spiritual exchange or conflict. The grace necessary for reconciling such conflicts must be fully fired in the crucible of awareness and choice. There can be no core minus that surrounding context which fulfills, not merely embroiders, its mission.

ọ

Of all the forgotten virtues, most lamented is lost irony. Today's battered youth, victim of the rapid obsolescence of goods and values, can only concentrate on the immediate task, or debt, or escape at hand. Meanwhile, imagination has been kidnapped by virtual reality and virtual junk. Bastardized, it reeks of the macabre and the meretricious. The language of classical music, its metaphysical journeys, its tender ironies, its endless correspondences of pattern, color, and imagery go wasting on brains that crave formulas and homogeneity. One thinks of the playing of Rachmaninoff, Cortot, Schnabel, a dynamic world of courage, range, and space.

ọ

By the seventh grade the constrictions of a deformed reality may have devastated the child's imagination. Processed information, garish imagery, received ideas, jellied maxims are orchestrated by the pseudo-rebellion of rock music, symmetrical response to the imposed world of fugitive trash. Thus the Minimalists, who offer an abbreviated mantra of sound to invoke the wonder of life in its simplest guises—a blade of grass or the rush of winds—indirectly try to restore the palliatives of myth. For without myth, the healing circuit between id and object, there is only black and white, yes and no, all the other great divides.

ọ

Original sin is indeed a vicious concept. Unfortunately it is true, in the sense of the universal failure to read the tea leaves, to acknowledge the facts of mortality and the damage done ourselves and others by cover-up of the original scar. So we hack away, repress and gorge, our greatest and most overt sins reserved for the rape of Gaea, the devastation of earth the mother: incest, the ultimate sin. The setting and arena of our dreams and abundance, of variety and equilibrium, the school of our imagination, the nursery to all powers of discrimination and fantasy, of color and grace, the cycle of being and its savior, moderation, is instead replaced by monstrous soap operas of envy and vengeance.

֎

That so much of contemporary art seems to deny or distort meaning, or to clothe it in ancient myths and cultures, is entirely understandable. Beyond these evasions and stratagems, which are the price of living in the twentieth century, to yet affirm faith, or the virtues of heroism and charity, is the province of a few whose superhuman will struggles against history. Yet, however magnanimous this effort, it remains in some way a Sisyphean task, built upon the given residue of twisted roots. For first the human mind must be detoxified, must acknowledge its fear and hubris, must repair its inner and outer scars. Until then, our best art will likely be either wistful fantasies of nature inviolate or stark portraits of nature and human nature violated, as rendered by meticulous ears and consciences.

֎

The doughnut, fresh for two hours before rigor mortis sets in, is the perfect emblem of the confection industry called entertainment. Its exquisite tautology of form, content of fat, and built-in obsolescence symbolize not only the disposable junk of pop culture but the ephemeral commodities of mall culture which swallow up our money and pride for their tokens of relief. Is it any wonder that young (and old) people can often no more think or speak? For the economy, its bromides and diversions, could not function without the manipulation and sabotage of our most reliable friend, language. And without language, its storehouse and circuitry, there is no thinking.

ọ

Of course there are bright young children who excel in science, music, law, and finance. I have taught them, and they are extremely smart—but not always intelligent. Like minicomputers, they process specific tasks with blinkered alacrity, yet they are woefully short of range and perspective. They lack the essential ingredients of a civilized (and musical) mind: pathos, irony, wit, patience, wonder. Instead they offer cynicism, blandness, facile idolatry, and ambitiousness. They are us, but a new and improved version which manages to be desperate without suffering, brittle without nostalgia. With equal parts anxiety and apathy we have trained them, until finally a sense of revulsion has begun to settle in and take hold. But whom shall we blame, the politicians or ourselves?

ọ

In the master class the students are invited to comment on performances by their colleagues. Much hesitation, much shyness. Is it a matter of not knowing the piece, of protecting the feelings of their friend, or of simple inability to phrase their thoughts? Mostly the latter, for the fecund language of music has no parallel in contemporary speech patterns, other than the serious works of fiction and poetry to which these young people are rarely exposed. The decriminalization of slang, sloganeering, huckstering, and doublespeak masquerading as intelligible communication has lobotomized the culture. What are left are sound bites, parodies, and paralysis, other than the recitations, always richly embroidered, of scandal and misery.

ρ̇

The number of speech categories available to youths seem limited to the following species: newsspeak, adspeak, politicalspeak, popspeak, and academicspeak. Newsspeak dispenses with context, proportion, and digression, the marks of cultivated thinking. Adspeak is premised upon ludicrous hyperbole and lies; it is the prototype of the debasement of language. Politicalspeak is a warmed-over version of adspeak. Popspeak has the grace of being rebellious and nihilistic, but dies by the weight of its dissociated reflexes. Academicspeak defines subject matter strictly according to internal reference segregated from alien allusions, thereby undermining the gift for metaphorical, figurative speech. The result of these various tendentious incursions on language is a desert of grunts, graphics, and graffiti or, at best, a spurious conciseness in the name of "clarity," which serves to make lies believable.

ρ̇

Variables are the curse of mankind. We generally acknowledge but two categories: us and them, acolyte and infidel, credo and discredited. Though acknowledging two, we believe in one, the other a wastebin of refuse, vice, heresy, and, above all, the unknown and the wicked, disparate confusion seething in its unholy womb.

Youth, the putative paragon of idealism and tolerance, has found and crowned the all-purpose term to deal with insidious variables. Unaware of its etymology, they tend to dub all imaginative or complex species of thought as "weird." If it is different, or strange, or old, or visionary, then it must be weird. But, on the other hand, if it is *wired*—i.e., graphically or electronically manipulated—

then it passes the Ivory test for being pure and natural. Rock and roll is not at all weird; it is monotonous, predictable, stagnant, and dreary.

ἀ

Ernest Jones, student and biographer of Freud, wrote a book about the various interpretations of *Hamlet* in which he made the following wise and valid observation. All the world is divided into two groups of people, those who divide the world into two groups and those who do not. The litany of fear, self-loathing, and rage behind this quintessentially human tendency to polarize experience has been well documented (and with special insight by Elias Canetti). Its manifestation in the field of music is devastating. All teaching, all criticism is subverted by the craven habit of making claims for a definitive method, a definitive performance. Equally atrocious is the glib and mundane practice of approving something simply because we like it, or rejecting it because we dislike it, as though personal taste, the laziest of barometers, were an index of universal standard.

ἀ

In an article denouncing the critic Ernest Newman for his condemnation of Strauss's *Elektra*, George Bernard Shaw makes the pertinent remark: "But he should by this time have been cured by experience and reflection of the trick that makes English criticism so dull and insolent—the trick, namely, of asserting that everything that does not please him is wrong, not only technically but ethically." As usual, Shaw neither minces nor misuses his words. Such criticism, chronic in the music profession at all levels, is dull precisely because the (un)chosen criterion is compulsively self-indulgent; it is insolent because it presumes that personal taste has more authority than the laws of art, which only the Muses can articulate and never do.

Previously the attempt to rationalize instinctual prejudices by clever argument and sophistry, a rather more refined display of intellectual pseudo-ethics, was more highly developed. This skill is no longer deemed necessary; the art or artist is either accepted or disposed of by subjective fiat.

ρ

In the days of sound bites, of strained gruel feeding on chronic restlessness, of violence as drugs and drugs as escape, what survives on the concert stage must be presented in brazen swaths of stark color (of which black and white are most highly prized), undiluted by the mixed hues and digressions of genuine poetry and fantasy. In the nights of Madonna and the casual juxtapositions of sacred and profane, audiences are bored unless the fare is familiar, labeled, glamorous. Of course there are dedicated listeners, often deemed "cultists," while an artist so labeled is doomed to marginal interest. The game is fame, while art remains a laborious maze.

ρ

Amusements and diversions have forever consoled and buttressed us against the grind of life. Worn down by spiritual, aesthetic, and economic deprivation, we splash our senses with the escapes and enchantments of fun and games, some genteel, some vicious. Of course, by contrast, no one can deny the spontaneous joy and lessons which issue from the games that children play, as Jean Piaget has so tenderly chronicled. But many historians and sociologists have wondered whether bread and circuses are the sop offered by the powerful to keep the common folk at bay, who are thus sufficiently pacified to forgo participation in the vital areas of community and self (ratio of actual to eligible voters in this country).

The phenomenon of rock music seems to me quite compatible with this theory. The current economic and psy-

chological insecurity, whether funk or malaise or spiritual
vacuum, calls forth a battery of therapeutic distractions.
Young people are especially vulnerable. While the chances
of making it in either the professional or the corporate
world gradually erode, the outlines and opportunities of the
information age remain, as of yet, more propaganda than
fact. The instinct to cry out, to bellow, to exult, to curse
this damned uncertainty is in every way understandable.
And the raging, Tantric character of much rock music
seems but a logical response to the chaotic, blackened environment which has spawned it.

That this musical revenge may be justifiable, however,
is only an incident in the larger chain of history, and in
the history of exploitation. For the real villains in this game
are the ones who have co-opted this resentment, merchan-
dised it, and turned it into platters of gold.

𝄢

There are several reasons which justify passionate commitment to the piano: (1) it offers familiarity with its great
literature; (2) it is endlessly puzzling and fascinating; (3) it
encourages one to be perpetually self-examining and self-
expressive at every level of the personality; (4) not least it
unmasks the wretched canard "prime of life"—for one gets
better and better.

This permanent quest for enlightenment is stonewalled
by the phenomenon of competitions. Young people, who
should have their whole lives to luxuriate in the feast of
great music and noble thoughts, are now condemned to an
iron curtain of likely rejection by the time they are thirty
or thereabouts unless they win some major award, itself no
guarantee of fame and the chances of which are microscop-
ically small.

There are several deleterious effects. Chief among them

is the cramping of repertoire by the need to present familiar works rehearsed and manicured over long stretches of time. The drive to explore, to identify the regions of the soul by unique choices of literature, is sacrificed to static routine and, as well, to a premature suavity which apes maturity by dissembling a solemn control in behalf of the fashionable aesthetic.

$\diamond$

Piano competitions have educated us to the dangers of a featureless musicality. For a surfeit of prize winners, as chosen by distinguished pedants, reflecting the virtues of their teachers by an obedient grooming of both phrase and drama, has shown us the futility of overly circumscribed approaches. The essential realms of grandeur and austerity, fantasy and asceticism have been leveled to a standard of pious, amiable discourse spiced with hot octaves and brilliant displays. But that may begin to change now, for there is nothing so tedious as musical playing—except for unmusical playing.

$\diamond$

The organisms of competitions and the network of managers and critics surrounding them are always lamenting the mediocre sameness of most winners. Their lament is self-deceiving, for they orchestrate the outcome.

There are three basic reasons why the results are so predictable: (1) The hierarchy represents and defends the prevailing aesthetic, despite the cries for an individual of striking, novel sensibility. Among other reasons, the system demands players who fit into the scheme of orchestral domination. (2) The winnowing process is prejudiced against poets and iconoclasts, who by definition disturb the tempo and the surface of the music, the twin inviolate categories about which the philistines are most vigilant. (3) For the

most part, the judges constitute a semipermanent tribe
wandering the capitals and upholding the consensus. They
know each other well, enjoy the responsibilities of influ-
encing the future of music, and share both their anecdotes
and dogmas of style. To borrow from Groucho Marx, any
club desiring such members is automatically unfit. For, beyond the threshold of basic standards, judging musicians is
like judging Miss America. In the end, cosmetics and in-
gratiation will win.

𝄽

As Bartók put it so succinctly, "Competitions are for
horses." Nothing could be more barbaric than the practice
of ranking artists as though they were divers or figure skaters. Even for such purely sporting activities, the criteria for
evaluation are often tentative to spurious. In music, that
most living and spontaneous of art forms, which Walt
Whitman, William James, and Kenneth Burke, among
others, have especially praised for having "no nay," the arbitrary classification of talent by rank is so unnatural as to
be the sign of pathological affliction. What one suspects is
that the appetite for dividing the world into winners and
losers, anointed and anonymous, is so compulsive that it
feeds with special, vindictive hunger on the most elusive
and ephemeral of subjects. For if music can be reduced to
games of power and success, then innocence—love without
profit—can be dealt a crushing blow.

𝄽

In a recent and excellent book about piano competitions,
my opinion of one of the finalists at a major event is quoted
without my knowledge, thus affording yet another of the
cryptic judgments so gratuitously indulged by the propri-
etors of the music profession. It is one thing to comment
upon an older, established artist, but to hang a presumably
authoritative label on the back of a developing artist is at

best cursory and at worst a damnation as permanent and ghostly as a shadow.

By what criteria and doctrines do we really know? And if we claim to know, is not a young performer entitled to various stages of growth and change? But the judgments themselves are so often fallacious and simpleminded. Can one dispute the ancient wisdom that all judgments invariably reflect more upon the judge than the victim? Is this not most conspicuously the case when addressing a subject so mercurial and complex as art? So mercurial and complex as youth?

ο

Opinions are a dime a dozen, and everybody has a right. The common wisdom rests in the conviction that the truth lies somewhere in the middle of the total mix, a formula by which figure skaters, divers, and gymnasts are evaluated.

Precisely. For, given the general practice of judging music competitions (as well as most auditions and examinations) by averaging out the point total, it is implied that musical performance is but another kind of athletic skill. Such a travesty of mixing apples and oranges betrays the impoverishment of most musical judgments.

To estimate a strong musical talent with fairness and insight demands cultivation, objectivity, and much modesty; to appraise less gifted performers requires even more sensitivity. Point totals are irrelevant. What matters is an attitude of support, subtle awareness, and blessing, while blunt criticism should be reserved only for those who are inordinately successful. (Yet even success, another kind of damnation, requires sympathy.)

ο

The hierarchy of all competitions issues the same cry—give us performers who will suspend our disbelief by the sheer force and uniqueness of their personality. When such candidates appear, however, they are invariably shot down.

A study printed in *Science News* (May 12, 1990) posits the criteria by which a group of college students evaluated standards of physical beauty. When given the choice between photographs of individual faces, however attractive, or composite pictures fusing sixteen or more different faces, the majority clearly identified the composite portraits as more representative of ideal beauty.

Ultimately, flawless beauty becomes banality. Contestants in a music competition who display "irregular" tendencies, who are restless, searching, vehement, angular, intellectual (above all!), despairing, ruminating, brazen— that is, who demonstrate all the qualities of music itself— are usually eliminated, sometimes with a guilty twinge, mostly with dispatch.

♩

A figure of considerable musical sophistication, who formerly worked in the management division of a major orchestra, once explained to me the rationale for awarding the first prize at an important piano competition she attended some years ago. It seems that the winner, by a charming tautology, had above all a "winning" smile and as well a "winning" way! What then could be more graphic evidence, more convincing proof of his winning gift? (Sic transit gloria.)

♩

Are competitions inherently dinosaurs and diversions? Yes, but it must conceded that a few of them have more humane ways and traditions. The Leventritt Award no longer entertains public jousts, but relies instead on private sources of research and recommendation. In similar fashion, the substantial Gilmore Awards are entirely decided by tapes and live concerts, dispensing with the mano-a-mano event while assuming a considerable burden of time, travel, and money. Then there is the competition sponsored by the Xerox Corporation through Affiliate Artists, which has the good grace and common sense to honor multiple winners (often four or five) with equivalent, unranked awards, thereby eliminating the danger of selecting only the most neutral specimen.

In the end all competitions are hostage to their level of judges and to the directorate which surrounds and appoints them. Very few of the most sensitive artists would dare or deign to serve in a role so contradictory to the axioms of their art.

ģ

Of the many mischiefs attending piano (and other) competitions, the prescription of mandatory repertoire is among the most egregious. Although this custom is finally ameliorating, the first round in many competitions still stipulates repertoire analogous to the compulsory school patterns required in figure-skating events: i.e., obligatory études, plus tokens of Bach and Beethoven or their surrogates. Thus technique is measured as an index of fast and efficient, as opposed to its valid function of servicing the palette of color and expression, while musicianship is authenticated by perfunctory and dutiful concessions to the hoary greats. For example, the conventional mentality which usually strangles Bach interpretations is so pervasive that a contestant who dared the true implications of the idiom would likely be cut or branded either a specialist or a crank. But those who safely oblige the pale injunctions of the day may remain within the pale.

ģ

Even more skewed than the usual pedantry of first-round requirements in competitions is the ritual of acknowledging the champion by display of a concerto performance in the final round. Any musician of reasonable experience would (or should) maintain that a major work of the solo repertoire is typically more revealing of essential, original talent than can be gleaned from most concerti. The reason is manifestly obvious: in a solo work one and only one is responsible for the total fabric of music and drama.

Of course the concerto experience has its own syndrome of difficulties, and is therefore plausibly included. But by placing it at the end of the competition and by weighting the vote in its behalf, the concerto becomes very much the public spectacle, reflecting the primacy of projection and theatrical command over musical values of intelligence and imagination. One must remember that the concerti which win competitions are typically *not* by Mozart, Beethoven, or Brahms—not to mention Schoenberg, Bartók, or Carter.

A simple compromise (as customary in the Queen Elizabeth competition): require a substantial solo work in conjunction with the concerto for the final-round offering.

₯

The world is filled with decent people who espouse material values in the name of "reality." For reality is so seductive, so chameleon a mistress, that one may feel quite ennobled while caving in to its imposing, if transient, demands. Thus the concerto, in particular the glamorous post-Romantic variety, becomes emblematic of the melodramatic soap operas which constitute our (imaginary) lives. By contrast, a large-scale Schumann work is commonly regarded as an interesting exercise in introspection bordering on neurosis, unsuitable for a general audience. That the Schumann may demand infinitely superior musicianship and vision is a proposition overwhelmed by the realities of the competition mystique and its ultimate muse, the box office.

Dominated by a wholly secular business climate, these are the values we teach our young. Most of them surrender and play the game without a whimper, so powerful is the reality principle.

ò

One stark and incontrovertible wedge of reality displays itself by the growing indifference of society toward serious music and the consequent decline of engagement opportunities for young musicians. The normal appetite for recognition is further exacerbated by a shrinking market. Young people, then, for reasons of survival while trapped in the noose of fading hopes, are more likely to shirk their ideals and to show more interest in professional road maps than in musical journeys.

Thus we have the phenomenon of gifted students who use rather than serve music.

ò

On the one hand, there is the spirit of rampant commercialism, personified by the elite manager who advised me that the Schumann Piano Concerto is no longer an effective public vehicle. On the other hand, there is the laughing gargoyle of the rock scene, anodyne and addiction for the young to soothe their grievances and sneer at the establishment. Both specters demand obedience and the forfeit of reflection. Both ensnare by the loud anvil chorus of bucks, decibels, and gratification. Both equate achievement with success, success with celebrity, celebrity with the demiurge of fame's embrace.

Competitions are a potent spur to this derangement of values. They bellow the siren song of instant success, a claim both fraudulent and unrealistic. They squelch the dreams of both winners and losers. They corrupt the sequence of eternal growth and the immaculate precept of lifelong loyalty to art.

It would be nice if all the teachers would get together and say *no más*. In the boxing ring it would be deemed cowardice; in musical circles it would be an act of noble defiance.

̦

Mea culpas are cleansing and, fortunately, freely available. My own students prepare for, attend, and often do well in competitions. My distaste for these circuses is tainted with hypocrisy, for I am a willing provider.

Nevertheless, there has been no failure to communicate my misgivings over the frailties of this game, alas the only game in town. My students know how skeptical I am of this mirage, this Medusa whose stare can freeze and deaden one's personality.

For no genuine authenticity can emerge in a pianist's character until years beyond the age deadline of most competitions. Before this deadline there is only a tug-of-war between a presentable facade and the struggle to assimilate endless and enigmatic amounts of material. In the meantime the student may feel compelled to play the game, but not without being advised of the hollowness of its motives and designs.

̦

As against the several insidious consequences of the competition scene, one redeeming blessing must be mentioned—the chance for most candidates to stay with gracious families who feed and nourish them for the duration. Such hosts provide a wonderful service in a spirit both generous and discreet. They offer a place to work quietly, and they offer heartfelt encouragement to the being and prospects of their talented guests. Similarly, the volunteers and auxiliaries of the competition give much tea and sympathy to the beleaguered contestants who, in their moment of agony, must compress a lifetime of commitment into a few minutes of Pavlovian exhibition.

These kind, hospitable souls are not unaware of the potential demoralization which may ensue from such traumatic events. But they dream that a star is being born—though often crossed, though often as sad as the story of Judy Garland.

҉

Nothing is more dreary or depressing than the raging, endemic split between intellect and feeling manifest in the general culture and sadly exemplified by the music business. How did these twin but indivisible faculties become so severed in the common (and critical) thought? The split is so mechanical that one wonders whether it is the consequence of purely biological distinctions between the two chambers of the brain. In the spiteful colloquy which follows, the intellect is generally the loser.

By the rebuke "intellectual," meaning heartless and calculating, composers such as Schoenberg and Sessions, pianists such as Schnabel and Brendel have been decried. The standard assumption contends that emotion and ecstasy are automatically excluded by the manipulation of cold, unfeeling systems.

This prejudice may be based upon an unconscious and curious misperception. Substitute "imagination" for "intellect," and the target becomes one more of fear than of loathing. For the educational system and cultural apparatus have been wholly deficient in their training of the imagination, other than in the varieties of kitsch. The deprived victims (and purveyors) of this inferior training, many of them in our conservatories, inevitably regard with suspicion and resentment those more fluent in the currency of the imagination, as well as those of more analytical intellect. But it is the imagination, the means for circumventing conventional thought, which is the more vulnerable target.

֍

The following extensive quote from George Bernard Shaw may provide healing and balm, plus sensible prescription, for the entirely ruinous dichotomy of intellect and feeling.

> *It is feeling that sets a man thinking, and not thought that sets him feeling. The secret of the absurd failures of our universities and academic institutions in general to produce any real change in the students who are constantly passing through them is that their method is invariably to attempt to lead their pupils to feeling by way of thought. For example, a musical student is expected to gradually acquire a sense of the poetry of the Ninth Symphony by accumulating information as to the date of Beethoven's birth, the compass of the* contra fagotto, *the number of sharps in the key of D Major, and so on, exactly analogous processes being applied in order to produce an appreciation of painting, Greek poetry, or what not. Result: the average sensual boy comes out the average sensual man, with his tastes in no discoverable way any different from those of the young gentleman who has preferred an articled clerkship in a solicitor's office to Oxford or Cambridge. All education, as distinct from technical instruction, must be education of the feeling; and such education must consist in the appeal of actual experiences to the senses, without which literary descriptions addressed to the imagination cannot be rightly interpreted . . . But in educational institutions appeals to the senses can only take the form of performances of works of art; and the bringing of such performances to the highest perfection is the true business of our universities.*

One could qualify this manifesto by the caveat that both categories, feeling and intellect, may mutually instruct, with neither of them necessarily prior, preeminent, or passive in the flow of the exchange.

ọ

It is plausible to locate imagination at the intersection of feeling and intellect. That is, feeling provides an emotional charge to the seamless spectrum of indistinct experience and generalized sensation detached from explicit identities or causes, such as dreams, landscapes vague or imaginary, states of elation or anxiety, et cetera; intellect presumably deduces cause and effect, provides categories, sequences, degrees of intensity, and whatever else may be subject to the analytical skills. Imagination crystallizes the broth of experience and the portions of observation into discrete images, giving them idiomatic names, emotional colorations, and modes of expression by which they are apprehended, described, and made singular.

In contemporary culture, the world of imagination has been debased, deformed, and literally prostituted. The roster of natural (or supernatural) imagery has been thoroughly co-opted by a pervasive advertising which fragments and subverts meaning, obliterating both mind and environment. Whatever imagery that might be regarded, by its heritage and quality, as innately appealing, proportioned, enchanting, consoling—the language of what is called "beauty"—has been purloined to sell off a variety of goods fraudulently adorned by stolen and distorted facsimiles of the beautiful.

ọ

The imaginative life retains its stamina, its authenticity, by examining experience with a dispassionate and impassioned innocence derived from curiosity and its attendant pleasures. But when experience, inner and outer, has been seized, garbled, and packaged to produce robotic messages and robots to watch them, curiosity is trampled and creativity flees to remote outposts. The characteristic youth of today—often so inarticulate, apathetic, anxious, explosive —is fashioned by forms of entertainment that monopolize attention, stun attentiveness, and dismantle the synapses of the mind.

It is not only churlish but preposterous to blame the young for the stupor that surrounds them and which they mirror so vividly. Their retreat to the dungeons of primordial grunting is not so much a march of the lemmings; it is more a response to the cultural environment, its brutalities, its man-made catastrophes, its vulgarity, most significantly the saturation of spurious sensations and factoids which become progressively meaningless or obsolete the instant after their birth. Without stability, guide, or direction, there are no roads out of the maze. Youth survives in a cave made bare and bearable only by the elimination of the mind and its constructs.

♀

Youths band together justifiably, in quasi catacombs which provide havens from the halting futility and hypocrisy of their adult supervisors. The adults improvise pseudo-answers which are then belied by their own confusion or indifference. Discipline is reserved only for the desperate need to survive in an economy which is constantly shifting the scope and nature of available jobs. The success of the economy depends upon the extent of consumer spending, often on products which are useless vanities and which have been designed more to hypnotize than to enlighten the personality.

The models of reading, of study, of curiosity, of exam-

ining the universe in its pageant of grandeur and delicacy
are practiced all too sporadically by the elders. The majority
are in no way ill-willed, but are victimized by the same
forces of instability and chaotic sensationalism so inimical
to defining decent values and reasonable limits. The garrulous world of Hydra-headed imagery, wherein advertising
and entertainment share identical motives and styles (with
"news" on the same path), precludes the staples of genuine
thought, contemplation, and critical analysis.

¿

All works of art, all varieties of entertainment have psychic and political themes. The presence of these themes is
inevitable, whether consciously intended or not. In kitsch
the appeal of these themes, however benign or insidious, is
directed toward a fundamental vulnerability of the soul in
its bias to absolutes and stereotypes. Thus the phenomenon
of Nazi and Soviet art; thus all stories and films which
glibly distribute the badge of good versus evil to their various characters; thus pop songs which croon more about the
miracle rather than the labor of love; thus the charms of
violence, horror, and comic books.

A simple index by which the value of a work of art can
be judged is the degree to which it avoids such obvious or
polemical appeals, as well as the degree to which it invites
reciprocal reflection. By this standard one could make the
following comparison.

In listening to the operas of Wagner, one is constantly
amazed by the fecundity of craft and invention. Nevertheless, any symphony of Beethoven is likely to be judged by
a still higher level of artistic integrity, ingenuity, and bold-
ness. The reasons can be ascribed to, if not reduced to, the
proposition that Wagner demands of the listener acquiescence. Beethoven demands awareness.

᷎

One observes the alarming decline in attendance of young people at concerts of classical music. Is there not a correlation between this phenomenon and a similar decline in the cognitive skills of our young? I would suggest that in both cases the missing ingredient is a natural and venturesome curiosity which extends over a range of ideas and subject matter. Intelligence itself is the casualty, and particularly imagination, for the energy of the thought process depends upon the seeding and collision of diverse materials drawn from various sectors of life. In that regard the feeble linguistic skills which our youngsters display is partly due to the generally casual requirements surrounding the study of foreign languages. The grammar, the diction, the sound, the idioms of vivid and unfamiliar languages provide a splendid source and counterpoint the better to appreciate the complexities of our own tongue. Nevertheless, the pernicious debasement of language is so consistent throughout the whole of society that we must remember it is the young who are the victims, not the perpetrators.

᷎

On a program some time ago of William F. Buckley's *Firing Line*, featuring a discussion about the reunification of Germany, some of the guests echoed an interesting linguistic bias, such that any proposal which appeared too idealistic, too visionary for the Realpolitik nature of the panel was dismissed as "romantic." But the ultimate seal of disapproval came from Henry Kissinger, who denounced one such "romantic" notion with the totally disabling epithet "poetry." Mr. Kissinger preferred a "sensible" approach.

Caution. How many lives have been lost and how much destruction wreaked by pursuing "sensible" policies? Which "sensible" are we talking about, the approach that proceeds inexorably step-by-step though oblivious to future consequences (Vietnam), or the one that implies a proportionate response to the just if contradictory demands of various needs and peoples?

May one also point out that the concept and content of poetry do not necessarily stand for caprice, exaggeration, and wishful thinking. Rather poetry embodies insight, concentration, discovery, thematic consistency, imagination, and wisdom, all healthy and sensible values to instill in our young people.

♭

The progressive division of America into a country of haves and have-nots, solvent and impoverished, elite and uneducated becomes a more salient fact with each passing day. From this condition it follows that but a limited pool of young people will have the means necessary to enjoy an extensive, costly, and varied education. Presumably our future leaders, however, will have access to the spectrum of ideas derived from a more comprehensive training and curriculum.

But this may not currently be the case. When I attended college in the late forties, the theory and category of a liberal arts major was not only available but considered desirable. Modern educational institutions, by contrast, prepare young people primarily for their economic livelihood. Specialization is the theme, from the academies to the professions. Even my home conservatory, a splendid school, has paid tribute to purely economic factors by instituting a *mandatory* one-year course in something called Career Management Skills, an understandable gesture reflecting both a betrayal of traditional educational ideals as well as the meager circumstances society offers to trained musicians.

♩

Lately there has been much talk of censorship, applied to such diverse expressions as a rap group, a comedian, a sculpture, some photographs, and a few flag burners. Anyone who breathes the spirit of American roots and values knows instinctively that censorship is the feeble response of an insecure, beleaguered society. However, that is no reason to sit on one's duff and not squawk loudly and protest vigorously when encountering something that is miserable and offensive.

But some works of art offend only to the degree we are unaware of their intent. Providing their level of craft is reasonably accomplished, works which are sharply provocative and polemical must be admitted to the dictionary of ideas (not to mention the open market).

♩

The imaginative life has been expropriated by two different but complementary forces: the Grand Guignol of contemporary culture and the laboratory of market research. The imagery of searing fantasy, delirium, the demiurge, and the cornucopia of color, myth, and libido have been neatly swiped by the entertainment business, which has transformed this vocabulary into a montage of reckless gratification and horror designed to stun its victims into uncritical numbness. A breathtaking symbiosis has formed between this tableau and the many insipid faces of advertising. The consumer is trapped between these twin overtures promising eternal youth, forgetfulness, and a teasing vortex of traumatic sensations. Every cheap myth of death, rebirth, and concupiscence is flaunted in a thousand cheap colors.

The uncoached, irresolute brain becomes putty for such clever snares. Youths pining for infancy and adults pining

for youth are the perfect pigeons for P. T. Barnum's famous
formula.

ọ

On the other side of the two cultures, science, sire to
space vehicles and all the formidable equations which detail
and expose the meaningful cycles of nature and man, has
contrived a prepossessing imagery which has intimidated
all the other professions, including art. From the incredibly
elegant designs (for instance, the fractal graphics illustrat-
ing the theories of Benoit Mandelbrot) to the playful grandeur of cosmological concepts, a daunting symbolism has
been created, decorative as a Miró, abstract as a Mondrian.

Unfortunately the theories and terminology of science are
not readily assimilated by the general culture, evidence of
which may be found in the projected shortage of thousands
of scientists in this country by the year 2000. It is not easy
to have conversations at cocktail parties or the family dinner
table about superstrings and quarks.

There are two other equally grievous by-products of the
ascendancy of science and its omnipotent stepchild, technology: (1) the actual and imaginative devastation of nature
as an arena for speculative fantasy; (2) the understandable
but craven mimicry of quasi-scientific methods by the other
professions.

ọ

To paraphrase Mendelssohn's cogent dictum, when compared to chronically ambiguous words, music is a far more
precise agent for articulating shades of meaning. Any musician worth his salt must believe this, must believe that
only music can describe the delicate interplay between subject and object which unlocks reality. And if the color of
the leaves which we may impute to a phrase in Schubert
may seem to vary from day to day, from performer to per-

former, so it varies in "reality," according to transient patterns of light, chemistry, and the moods of the observer.

For some, the leaves may compound into characteristics of bark or moss. For others, into clouds or cherrystone clams. But the essential quality remains, and is of a character which is neither subject nor object but rather the product of the eye and of recognition fully concentrated. Nor is this quality derived from (or perjured by) the vagaries of temperament alone; instead its author is the process of mind projecting identity and worth onto putatively neutral objects (but with distinct properties).

The shortage of fantasy in modern performance and criticism is a function of limited attention to the artifacts of man and nature. As disposable merchandise becomes our daily provender, Rilke's observation that his generation would be the last to know "things" becomes ever more poignant.

ρ

There are two kinds of critical judgments, fallible and fallacious. The people who take on this role professionally place themselves in a dangerous position, ready to be snubbed not only by history but by the protagonists on the front line of creation. The terrible cross to be borne comes down to the fatal truism: Nothing is easier than to criticize.

If judgments are to be made, then presumably the judge should be more learned, more virtuous than the work or artist to be judged. No preconceptions, hand-me-downs, shallow systems, stylistic pigeonholes, or the propaganda of tradition should contaminate the sympathy of mind necessary to identify with the plot and fate of the artwork. What is the artist trying to do? And how can one encourage artists to be spirited, sane, magnanimous?

For we are all critics, and if one tallied up the poison

against the promise we have spread, there are likely more cramped than liberated souls out there. Disorderly habits and indifferent standards should not be condoned, but the secret of their redemption lies not in excoriation but in claiming their juices for nobler missions.

ℓ

In the typical urban landscape which is home to most advanced students of music, their physical and metaphysical companions are for the most part noise, grime, traffic, the behemoth skyscrapers which dominate sunless streets, beggars, bag ladies, the homeless, the whole panoply of driven and derelict society, hypocrisy, and injustice. What is comfortable, elegant, and fashionable lies beyond the student's price range, and often beyond the bounds of good taste (atriums and malls). There is solace in the hot-dog vendor, the boutiques for cheese and sushi, jeans and shades, the neurotic squirrels hustling the curbs, the crummy theaters showing old movies. There is solace in the museums, parks, and libraries. There is solace in each other, struggling and hoping, trying to figure out the game, waiting for reinforcements to prop up old and frayed ideals. And there is solace in music, despite its illusory path as the ladder to success (but mostly to failure).

From this environment, better or worse according to one's quota of resiliency, must grow the Elysian fields of musical majesty and expression. It works best if you believe that sensory deprivation stimulates the senses.

ℓ

Certain trends in the media display and feed the most sorrowful features of human nature. An addiction to sports, the bane and sweet tooth of my life, has made me an expert on one of those trends. I refer to the habit, more and more prevalent, of concentrating the camera on the face of the *loser*, the player who just struck out, or let in the winning goal, or lost the match. Meanwhile the winner, who parades his sportsmanship by jumping up and down like a monkey with a hotfoot, shaking his fist at the heavens to thank or defy Destiny, is given more perfunctory treatment. The camera prefers to dwell on the gaunt faces of the vanquished, which reflect anything from stoic rigidity to lacerating anguish. Our appetite for misery, for peering at those whom we denigrate yet identify with, has collapsed all standards of balance. The TV director more than obliges, reminding us with a flourish of our fascination with loss and morbidity. The loser-as-pariah becomes the release and therapy of our own salvation.

Moral: People who are starved of spirit, art, and landscape turn anxiously to and upon each other for that charge and vindication which alone they cannot summon.

♭

The newspapers, the magazines, the tube, all media outlets have joined in a rite of passage unthinkable a few years ago. Apparently it is not sufficient to compile spurious lists of the ten best of everything; now the feeding frenzy demands and relishes the ten worst. What a pathetic display of peacock braggadocio, of vulgar chortling over the presumed defects and miseries of the accused. What an infantile betrayal of journalism, based upon the pitiful rationale of giving the people what they want: wimpy, craven copout.

On the sports pages they now list the worst of the week, a further refinement. The latest horror, however, is the slimy practice of the reporter providing grades for each player at critical junctures of the season, as though he were the teacher filling out report cards.

Yes, we know that the players are paid exorbitant salaries, and that taking some shots goes with the territory.

But, apart from the compromise of dignity and decency, how can an amateur observer presume absolute, finite judgment when the skills involved are so complex and pressured? A little modesty and fairness, please. A little common sense.

ρ

Milan Kundera once observed in an article for *The New York Review of Books* that one attraction of Lawrence Sterne's *Tristram Shandy* lay in its disregard for conventional formal principles. To wit, after the first introductory page, the next ninety-nine pages wander off on a complete detour from the basic plot. By all ordinary perspectives, such a digression should totally subvert the sense and structure of any coherent form. It is precisely the fact and nature of this digression which Kundera finds so appealing.

All works of art possess a network of themes and meanings corresponding to the central convictions of the work. For analysts, performers, and teachers, the trick is to evaluate the comparative significance of the various elements. The persistent danger is that by asserting too rigidly what is foreground, essential, and preeminent, the middle ground and background material may seem by contrast less important, less worthy of attention. For if one concentrates too much on the "big picture," there may finally be no picture at all, or only the shell of one. The foreground elements may be more conspicuous, but they are not necessarily more important. The rotations and displacements of foreground and background materials and the elaborate pathways between them are intrinsic to our modes of seeing and hearing. Sensitivity to these supple relationships should be cultivated, not stoned by reductive theories.

ρ

In the dubious practice of student evaluation of the faculty which many educational institutions currently condone, there is one standard question which is prone to exercise the wrath of most students. How well does the teacher organize his materials? The presumed inability of the teacher to parcel out relevant information in perceptible and conventional sequence becomes grounds for condemnation and divorce. The student will always want the key facts relayed in discernible, abbreviated progression, the better to assert his command of the material upon examination.

It is not unreasonable to seek out the identity of those central themes outlining the subject matter. It is, however, naive, superficial, and grossly utilitarian to extract forcibly such themes from their developing and qualifying context. Things have meaning only in their relation to other things, and to abbreviate, digest, or obliterate the mother lode of allusions is to apply a tourniquet to the central themes, turning them into frozen clichés.

As in Jean Genet's dramas, neither icons nor worshippers, master symbols nor sideshows can survive one without the other.

ò

In his book *Patterns of Nature*, Peter Stevens contends that "meandering" itself is one of the elemental patterns persistently replicated in the natural world. For humans, meandering is a term of obloquy, a condition of vagrancy, a sign of irresponsibility. Such an aimless attitude goes against the grain of all the instincts and homilies of a linear, additive, economy-bound social psychology. Thus, if it doesn't grow, it's dead.

But it turns out that meandering is one of nature's solutions to the condition and context of dynamic variables. When the entire ecology of wind and rock, ground and vegetation is involved, then streams will meander to accommodate their purposes for and within the surrounding environment.

And so the work of art proceeds, nor is it only Schubert who meanders. The music of the supreme architect, Bach, is filled with pages of discursive argument and rumination, glorifying the nameless whole by a rich embroidery of passages which lead everywhere and nowhere. The ideas are presented, stood on their head, dissolved into fragments, until the ultimate message becomes the connection of all things great and small, a chain of being which cannot be secured until the last note is in place.

There are no ghettos in the work of art. The lowliest worm and wormwood have a place at the banquet table.

♩

The music of Arnold Schoenberg is consistently described (and derided) as the product of a neurasthenic intellectual whose complex structures defy both coherence and pleasure. The discovery and use of the twelve-tone method of composition (for Schoenberg, an inevitable development of the destabilization of tonality) is regarded as a symptom of several deadly diseases, including megalomania, latent communism, and brain distention leading to a withered heart.

The reason that critics and audiences do not cozy up to the music of Schoenberg is not because it is so intellectual but because it is so emotional. As he writes in a letter to Busoni, he tries to compose a music which would reflect the intense and contradictory dialogue of our psychological life: thoughts subverting thoughts, feelings, images; ideas spinning in a kaleidoscope of sensations; everything emotionally charged. The organization of such diverse material is possible only through the mind of an experienced craftsman classically trained and through the ear of an inspired chemist of sound.

All our native predispositions in favor of black and white gang up against this artist of vivid sensibility whose music summons up more the risks of a churning sea than the pleasures of a tepid bath.

♀

When Beethoven made sharp response to a letter from his brother Karl, who embellished his signature with the phrase "land-owner," the composer added "brain-owner" to his own autograph.

The semiconscious prejudice against manifest intelligence in music and performance is quite staggering. The public wants to be soothed, caressed, dazzled, and it especially appreciates the stock travails of a wounded heart. The critics also like their music digestible and well labeled, for they are beholden to set prescriptions of style and, therefore, show discomfort, even petulance, when a performance collapses their naive categories.

If one could reveal the full implications of the music, its sources, sorceries, and prophecies in addition to the appropriate idioms, the majority of critics and public alike would be at best thoroughly mystified and at worst angered by the violation of their received ideas. If one truly understood music, as a parable of ideas, legends, portents unfolding in a scheme of both self-reference and metaphor, then intellect would not be regarded as suspiciously unmusical. And imagination would stand for something besides pretty colors.

♀

At the end of the '80s decade there were several broadcast programs featuring panels of distinguished citizens offering impressions of the past decade and predictions for the future one. Redeeming aspects of the social condition were not easy to come by, but one author observed that the most tangible sign of hope she had seen was the picture of young people on a beach patiently cleaning the feathers of birds who were mired in an oil slick.

How right she is. How satisfying to see this gesture of kindness, and to know that the light of caring shines within these youths who eventually will be custodians of the earth and of the species who share it with us. Perhaps it is my delusion, but somehow I cannot visualize these samaritans, in applying their hands and hearts to the grim task, accompanied by wailing boom boxes.

Serious music is losing the young generation, and unless we wake up, the next decade will see most concerts confined to private salons. Fortunately, the lust for idealism is imperishable, and perhaps the green revolution and the movement in behalf of animal rights are its gentle harbingers.

ɋ

Goethe confessed that there was no crime committed on earth of which he was not capable.

If we applied that presumption universally, the education of our young people would be far more insightful and appropriate. There is no great mystery here; we are just too afraid to look directly within, to see the scarrings which cover our psychic wounds and contradictions. All the insane militarism of this and other centuries is caused by pathetic bluff and counterbluff. People weak and strong feel inadequate, therefore victimized, therefore hostile, therefore murderous. The exercise of power is only by corollary an aphrodisiac; primarily it is an escape from truth, the truth of an endemic insecurity which is the flip side of the dangerous move to acquire consciousness. As soon as we became aware of decay and mortality, we pillaged and murdered and drank the blood of our enemies to replenish the constantly failing supply of self-esteem and divine support.

We call it the "dark" side, but we have made it dark. If we instructed children on life and death, if we portrayed the cycle as grand and shared, if flora and fauna were our intimate companions, if we provided work that challenged both hands and mind, then we would have wiser and stronger children—and better musicians.

◊

The eternal now of modern culture is more to be mourned than condemned. It is the result of a historical process mostly defined by the exponential growth in communications technology. Human beings retreat into a conspiracy of self, pandering to every whim and disturbance of their battered sensibilities. Songs, movies, TV, fiction and nonfiction all revel and mire in the same theme, the inadequacy and pathos of man's fate—and how to fix it. Poor, miserable, disheveled humanity: we stare at it and bemoan the pathetic cycle of hope and disaster. Like any subject explored obsessively, the tale becomes wretched and tedious.

Man, the spokesman of god and nature, is now a patient in his own sanitarium, dying of terminal anxiety and boredom. Unable to accept mortality, or fallibility, or the whimsy and mystery of the gods, we lance our sores, looking for imaginary demons, and plaster the wounds with Band-Aids in decorator colors.

It is time to remember that we are but a fraction of the universe, and that it is our mission and privilege to engage it. It is time to acknowledge that human beings have limits and are therefore, a priori, of limited interest.

◊

In poetry there is sound and rhythm; in painting there is line and color; in sculpture there is shape and form; in prose there is composition; in architecture there is "frozen music"; in dance and film, music is the essential context. Music is but one of the arts, but it lives in all of them. Music is directed toward the ear but appeals indirectly to all the senses and their mental counterparts. Music is the art to which all other arts aspire.

Music and art overlap, but are not the same. A performance may be wholly musical, but inartistic or distant from artistic impulses. A performance may be wholly artistic, but unfaithful to musical considerations. Which is more significant, the art or the music?

The question is thorny, divisive, perhaps artificial, creating sides and potential conflicts awkward to explore. But one asks it in order to find an approach which may gather both the musical and artistic threads into some double helix of exchange. And one asks it to apprehend a curious phenomenon—how can so many just, virtuous, and sensitive performances be yet so lame or devoid of artistic merit, of the special ruses and flights of imagination which provide insight and mystery?

ô

In music we may play the notes with meticulous care; we may arrange them to conform with the laws of phrasing; we may balance them to conform with the laws of acoustics and voicing; we may connect and relate them judiciously to oblige the patterns of form and development; we may pay strict attention to all existing signs of notation, dynamics, and expression.

In doing so, we win our stripes as exemplars of musical fidelity. We are respected by audiences and professionals, perhaps even gaining prominent careers. We are noble soldiers in behalf of our craft, and thus we may hope to be admitted to the blessed guild and service with the angels. But we are not artists.

ọ

According to Pierre-Auguste Renoir, there are two indices of genuine art: it is inimitable, and it is ineffable. Mr. Steuermann gave it a different twist when he observed that the two things one cannot teach are "culture" and "atmosphere." Regardless of who makes the case, the indefinability of artistic presence and character is an axiom of criticism and teaching.

But that does not prevent us from trying, however vainly, to define it. Or at least from honoring this mysterious emanation which charges or sacralizes the rare work, the rare performance. One may well concede—Yes, I cannot define it, but I know it when I see it, when I hear it. As though art were some distant cousin of obscenity, equally elusive and no less indebted to Eros.

Still, for selfish reasons, I would try to fathom the sources. For it's my hope to work with students who have the chance of becoming genuine artists as well as faithful musicians. I want to know how to stir up and communicate this elusive property. But my colleagues caution—the student either has it or doesn't. Being an unregenerate skeptic, I seek out the traces, though aware that this "ineffable, inimitable" quality may only briefly be touched before it wiggles away. But for a pianist, touch is everything.

ọ

The bemusing reality is that recognition of art does not, in fact, yield to the test for obscenity devised by Potter Stewart, in that we may not know it when we see it. Significant art, past and present, has been set before connoisseurs, critics, and public, only to be, on more occasions than not, ignored and condemned. For art may make an impression so vague or radical, so ungainly or diffuse, that it tumbles right by, leaving us mystified or irritated. Why this happens is a matter of speculation, but surely it is somehow related to the distance between the fashionable norm and the artistic challenge. For what is reliably good and what is mysteriously great are on different tracks. (Voltaire: "The best is the enemy of the good.")

The touch of genius required to transcend the merely competent is articulated in Goethe's aphorism: "The artist who is not also a craftsman is no good; but, alas, most of our artists are nothing else." Craft is the essential prerequisite, but it is not enough. In piano playing today, for example, it is plausible to assert that never have we had so many pianists playing on such a high level of technical facility and brilliance. It is equally true that never before have so many paid such relatively careful attention to the indications of the text. But it is debatable whether both of these honorable developments have led to a greater incidence of art.

♭

The quest for serenity and sanctuary in an environment prone to violence, to violations of privacy and sanity, to relentless assaults on one's senses and values becomes an ever real and persistent craving. For those of us addicted to serious art, perhaps only odes to butterflies, to deities, to blades of grass can settle our frazzled nerves. For apparently the public is turned off by those complex artworks which would reveal the dense, ironic layers of meaning that constitute reality.

As artists, are we quasi psychiatrists who mend the soul? Do we provide the consolations, escapes, and reassurances which enable us to survive? Or are we reporters of the truth, assembling the multiple shards of reality into intricate portraits which seek out the connections between misery and blessing, violence and wisdom? Do we protect or investigate the heart?

҉

One begins to root for the tennis players who have the fewest logos and advertisements crawling, like fungus, over their outfits. (They are pikers compared to racing drivers and their vehicles.) The sporting arena itself is plastered with the garish colors of goods begging for homes, as though they were raucous and abandoned pups waiting for disposal at the pound. The urban environment has become a continuous billboard, intruding into every human activity previously inviolate, until freedom itself becomes the ward and stepchild of desirable goods.

Commercial products are overtly and covertly advertised in films—for a quid pro quo. Movies and commercials intermarry, news and entertainment breed like rabbits, concert series as well as golf tournaments are named for their sponsors. To endorse a product becomes the ultimate goal for public figures.

In this atmosphere the few remaining athletes who disdain endorsements and who refuse cash for their autographs deserve sainthood. In this atmosphere, where the world of color and romance has been glazed over, blown up, vultured, and shredded, the child's imagination must be restructured with utmost care.

҉

The personality of sports has changed dramatically and in rather disillusioning, demoralizing ways. It is not only the infusion of money which has altered the guidelines and the headlines but the change in tempo, strategy, and profile which has undermined the character of several sports. For instance, professional basketball has outlawed a legitimate defensive alignment (the zone defense) in order to speed up play. The game has deteriorated into a monothematic display of individual skills, which become necessary to oblige the twenty-four-second limit on possession. The result is a kaleidoscope of supremely inspired hysterics and scrambles, as though watching rabid greyhounds pursue an imaginary rabbit.

Sports like football and ice hockey progressively emphasize brawn over finesse, restricting not only certain possibilities of deployment and strategy but also the roster of key players ever more liable to injury. Even a game like tennis has partly succumbed to the influences of power and speed, so that artists like Sergi Brugera and Miloslav Mecir, Michael Chang and Henri Leconte seem to wither under the fusillade of their aggressive, ball-pounding opponents. The game has become less interesting, the rackets larger, the players clones and slaves to the model of heavy serve and topspin. Particularly in women's tennis the stereotype prevails.

Baseball, despite its artificial designated-hitter rule, remains an ideal equation of skill and machination, action and thought. As long as there is baseball the country can be saved, even if the hot dogs are greasy and undercooked.

♭

As a chronic and condemned Dodger fan, baptized in Dodger blue before I was ten (after a brief infantile fling with the Yankees), I well remember the great teams of the '40s and '50s. The names and deeds of marvelous players resound in my private hall of fame. They were players of spectacular ingenuity, players with imagination who were sly and inventive, and they played in parks throughout the league which were unique in personality and conformation.

For instance, the outfield of Crosley Field in Cincinnati actually slanted upward as it approached the fence! Unimaginable by today's homogeneous standards.

There was Pistol Pete Reiser, an outfielder of incredible energy and fire, in the style of Mickey Mantle, who played with a bravado few modern players or pianists can match. He ruined his career by smashing into outfield fences trying to catch long fly balls. He also had a great arm, a gift I have always admired in outfielders. Therefore I had a special fondness for Carl Furillo, the Dodger right fielder, who was known as the Reading (Pa.) Rifle. I would come to the park early to watch the outfield practice, just to see Furillo show off his magnificent arm. It was as though he had incredible octaves, or could play the leaps in the Schumann Fantasy with amazing nonchalance and speed.

♩

Duke Snider was the center fielder. He played with a special grace, bearing, and resilience. I will never forget an important catch he made in Shibe Park, Philadelphia, climbing the wall in left centerfield to snare a long drive off the bat of Puddin' Head Jones. The shortstop was Pee Wee Reese, a man of all seasons and the glue that held the team together. He could field, he could hit more than his share of home runs for a middle infielder, and he knew the subtle intricacies of the game, the fourth dimension. At crucial and unexpected times (with two out and a runner on third base) he would lay down a bunt for a base hit, an art almost totally forgotten in a day of statistics and stereotypes. He was also the gracious Southerner who befriended Jackie Robinson, smoothing the otherwise turbulent entry of the first black accepted into major league baseball.

Jackie Robinson was Hermes the Thief incarnate. Of

phenomenal speed and cunning, although a big man who played college football, he accomplished things as a base runner that no one has ever seen, before or since. I refer not only to his spectacular gift for stealing home, but for impromptu moves which confounded the opposing team (and the crowd) by an uncanny timing which was both daring and unpredictable. The gift transferred, he would have played Chopin and Liszt with an astonishing spontaneity worthy of these magical poets. The audience would be amazed and enlightened.

ò

In the '40s the feared rivals of the Dodgers were the St. Louis Cardinals, a team of colorful players with fantastic talents. I have never seen a player of such concentrated and effortless grace as Stan Musial, an outfielder–first baseman whose swing uncoiled in a continuous purposeful arc. The great god of performance, from dancing to piano playing to baseball, demands one property common to all, coordination, of which Musial was the ideal embodiment. More than that, his casual elegance for the game, in the style of Fred Astaire, both belied and occasioned his remarkable stamina and focus.

Also on the Cardinals was Terry Moore, a Douglas Fairbanks kind of centerfielder; Marty Marion, the "Octopus," whose fielding skill and range justified his nickname; Enos "Country" Slaughter, among the most aptly named athletes in history; hard-rock Mort Cooper, pitching to his brother, Walker Cooper, who described the catcher's implements (mask and padding) as the "tools of ignorance."

And then there was the ultimate artist among pitchers, Howie Pollet, whose refinement of his craft was something akin to that of the pianist Dinu Lipatti. Only an aficionado would understand, but Pollet could throw change-of-paces off his basic change-up, giving him a bewildering variety of speeds all delivered with a perfect *legato* motion. His counterpart on the Dodgers was another southpaw, Elwin "Preacher" Roe, who pitched the way Walter Brennan acted, with savvy and rustic cunning.

◊

Among my favorites on the Dodgers of those years were players of genuine personality with wonderfully quirky names to match: such as Cookie Lavagetto, Dixie Walker, Goody Rosen, Babe Phelps, Dolf Camilli, or the "Bounding Basque," Pete Coscarart. Then there was Eddie Basinski, a wartime second baseman who, during the winter off-season, played in the violin section of the Buffalo Philharmonic!

I was especially taken with a pitcher from that team, a skilled and determined craftsman who, for me, owned a magically mellifluous name, Whitlow Wyatt. All these names and games came alive through the agency of one voice, Red Barber, who was the radio announcer for the Dodgers. It may seem peculiar or paradoxical to confess, but in my childhood Red Barber was very much a moral guide, by virtue of his example of reason in the face of passion, tolerance of both fate and hated rivals, pervasive courtesy as the price of civilization, and a gentle but stirring eloquence which made the routine seem poetic and rejuvenating. You could always smell the fresh grass and the roasted peanuts through his musical voice of magnolia charm and decency. There was nothing of this tragic sense of doom, grim and dour, leading to our usual hyperbolic flights of hope, angst, paranoia, and snap judgments. Red Barber was a gentleman with a colorful eye. He taught me a great deal about sportsmanship and dignity.

◊

In its present incarnation, sports is full of insidious deeds and attributes: greed, petulance, cheating, cheerleaders, AstroTurf, braggadocio, agents, jingoism, and gross hyperbole—perhaps the biggest sin because it always demands more and gives less.

Nevertheless, sports can approximate art, and some of its performers are true artists who redeem sports from its current narcissism and hysteria. They are artists by virtue of their skill, their imagination, and their adherence to a performance ideal immeasurably more significant than the rewards. And some, who may not be artists, are yet gentlemen and gentlewomen who embody standards of sportsmanship and decency.

Art challenges, sport celebrates. Both entertain, but the artist, by transcending his culture, will always discover new standards of meaning and doing. The true sportsman, through disinterested play, reflects the human condition by acknowledging dignity as superior to winning.

♪

The dualistic way of thinking, with all its frigid dichotomies, must inevitably be apprehended and confronted before pathways to reconciliation and enlightenment can be found. And, indeed, these pathways are themselves deceptive, for the burdensome division of consciousness into subject and object can never be refuted, only ameliorated. As artists, as humans, we cannot escape this permanent exile from the world of objects; we can only endure this melancholy condition by peering ever more sympathetically into the storehouse of fugitive things and beings, while extolling their variety and sorcery.

In a book called *Letters on Cézanne*, which should be required reading at all conservatories, Rilke describes the "limitless objectivity" which Cézanne exemplifies: "this labor which no longer knew any preferences or biases or fastidious predilections, whose minutest component had been tested on the scale of an infinitely responsive conscience, and which so incorruptibly reduced a reality to its color content that it resumed a new experience in a beyond of color, without any previous memories." By surrendering entirely to the character of the object, personality is reborn through the act of seeing, of watchfulness. And the bearer of this gift, emptied of prejudice, becomes reality's faithful and singular correspondent, identifiable through the mission of careful study.

ọ

My teacher assigned a prelude by Debussy entitled "Bruyères." I asked him for the meaning of the term *bruyères*, and he suggested that it was something like heather. As a deprived city boy, I did not know either the quality or the look of heather; but now it is time to redeem my ignorance by citing Rilke's description from his book on Cézanne, in which the author is responding to a letter from an intimate friend.

> *Never have I been so touched and almost gripped by the sight of heather as the other day, when I found these three branches in your dear letter. Since then they are lying in my Book of Images, penetrating it with their strong and serious smell, which is really just the fragrance of autumn earth. But how glorious it is, this fragrance. At no other time, it seems to me, does the earth let itself be inhaled in one smell, the ripe earth; in a smell that is in no way inferior to the smell of the sea, bitter where it borders on taste, and more than honeysweet where you feel it is close to touching the first sounds. Containing depth within itself, darkness, something of the grave almost, and yet again wind; tar and turpentine and Ceylon tea. Serious*

*and poor like the smell of a begging monk and yet again
hearty and resinous like precious incense. And the way
they look: like embroidery, splendid; like three cypresses
woven into a Persian rug with violet silk (a violet of such
vehement moistness, as if it were the complementary color of
the sun). You should see this. I don't believe these little
twigs could have been as beautiful when you sent them:
otherwise you would have expressed some astonishment
about them. Right now one of them happens to be lying on
dark blue velvet in an old pen and pencil box. It's like a
fireworks: well, no, it's really like a Persian rug. Are all
of these millions of little branches so wonderfully
wrought? Just look at the radiance of their green which
contains a little gold, and the sandalwood warmth of the
brown in the little stems, and that fissure with its new,
fresh, inner barely-green.*

Now I think I know what heather is. Perhaps. On the
other hand, Mr. Steuermann told me the story of a man
trying to describe the character of milk to his blind friend
(a similar story can be found in a 1934 letter by Arnold
Schoenberg to Walter E. Koons, music supervisor of
NBC):

> *"Simple, to start with, it's white."*
> *"But what is white?" his friend asks unavailingly.*
> *"And besides, it is a liquid, like water."*
> *"But what is water?"*
> *"Look here, it is white, and it is a smooth, creamy
> liquid that comes from a cow."*
> *"But what is a cow, and what is smooth and creamy?"*
> *"Well, let's put it this way, it is like rubbing your
> hand along the neck of a swan."*
> *"Ah! Now I know what milk is."*

$\wp$

One more quotation from Rilke's study on Cézanne, a magnificent description affirming the interdependence of all of the separate parts of a work of art, affirming the divinity and significance of each detail, however minute.

> *In the brightness of the face, the proximity of all these colors has been exploited for a single modeling of form and features: even the brown of the hair roundly pinned up above the temples and the smooth brown in the eyes has to express itself against its surroundings. It's as if every place were aware of all the other places—it participates that much; that much adjustment and rejection is happening in it; that's how each daub plays its part in maintaining equilibrium and in producing it: just as the whole picture finally keeps reality in equilibrium. For if one says, this is a red armchair (and it is the first and ultimate red armchair ever painted): it's true only because it contains latently within itself an experienced sum of color which, whatever it may be, reinforces and confirms this red . . . Everything has become an affair that's settled among the colors themselves: a color will come into its own in response to another, or assert itself, or recollect itself . . . In this hither and back of mutual and manifold influence, the interior of the picture vibrates, rises and falls back into itself, and does not have a single unmoving part.*

Correspondingly, each note of the musical text belongs to and qualifies all the other and sum of the notes; their hierarchy of values, defining which are the more or less important notes, constitutes but a single, limited perspective for entry into the forest, which itself cannot flourish without the contributions of the lowliest leaf or insect. The overview is fallacious absent the scrutiny of all those minute sounds and their connections. Perhaps that is why they are called grace notes.

𝄞

In his remarkable book *The Tuning of the World*, the Canadian composer R. Murray Schafer chronicles the history of our sound environment from ancient Greece to the present. It is not a pleasant story. Our first companions in the chamber music of the planet were the voices of the sea, the multiple incarnations of wind and water, and the murmurings and groanings of earth, vegetation, and forest. These voices were mysterious but somehow reassuring; they gave evidence and credence to our quest for the divine origins of life.

From a variety of ancient and modern sources, poets and historians, Schafer documents a litany of natural sounds appealing to our ears, caressing our senses, satisfying the soul. One fervent example was offered by Stravinsky, who characterized what he loved most about his homeland as "the violent Russian spring that seemed to begin in an hour and was like the whole earth cracking." Schafer compares this primal song and its evolution through hunting and rural societies to our contemporary environment, our world of "sound imperialism," where "the slop and spawn of the megalopolis invite a multiplication of sonic jabberware." Anything goes; sound is power, street noise and machine noise are deafening and ubiquitous, the ears degenerate, the mind is a punching bag for the sirens of commerce and come-ons. Is it any wonder that Schafer concludes his book with a humble plea for silence?

♭

Several years ago the great pianist Alfred Brendel was a guest on one of the more literate national TV shows. The interviewer asked Brendel for his feelings and attitude toward the audience. The reply was straightforward and amusing. To paraphrase, Brendel said that, above all, he wanted the audience to *listen*; and then he pointed out, with impish pride, that "listen" is an anagram of "silent." Much chuckling then, and a look of pleasant consternation on the interviewer's face.

On the subject of silence, Schafer's book identifies an alarming linguistic bias. Many synonyms of the term *silent* have uneasy and negative connotations. They include: *mute, speechless, sullen, saturnine, taciturn, reticent, inarticulate,* and other samples of suspect behavior. What a peculiar, frightened condition prevails when the simple absence of sounds, words, or noise suggests modes of disagreeable or pathological derangement. We must *communicate*; that is the cri de coeur of every expert on the human condition. Communicate what? What is there to say until we have listened, faithfully listened, to sounds and words of substance, of meaning?

Without silence there is no music. Not simply because the faculty of hearing deteriorates from constant exposure to noise, but because silence is both the majestic frame and the stable solution for musical (and poetic) ideas. Silence is the soda water, the bracing ether, the bridge and mode of respect for receiving instructions from the angel. Or as wise Schnabel described his own gift, other pianists played the notes more perfectly, but nobody could play the rests better.

♩

Emerson wrote a poem that speaks poignantly to the issues of beauty and truth, the elevated and the commonplace, the noble and the dark sides. It is titled simply "Music."

> Let me go where'er I will
> I hear a sky-born music still:
> It sounds from all things old,
> It sounds from all things young,

From all that's fair, from all that's foul,
Peals out a cheerful song.

It is not only in the rose,
It is not only in the bird,
Not only where the rainbow glows,
Nor in the song of woman heard,
But in the darkest, meanest things
There alway, alway something sings.

'T is not in the high stars alone,
Nor in the cup of budding flowers,
Nor in the redbreast's mellow tone,
Nor in the bow that smiles in showers,
But in the mud and scum of things
There alway, alway something sings.

Plainness, darkness, roots, salamanders, stones, moss, grains have their music too. Not sounds of celestial beauty; nor the indulgent, plastic mimicries of love, the light and heavy metal of futile abandon. More like the sounds of serious contemporary music, where Orpheus meets the Druids, where star, soil, and turbulent sea mingle in some witchcraft of cubism redeemed, a kind of "concord" sonata in which concord and discord are resolved by their faith in things as they are, as they were, as they were meant to be. It would be nice if people really listened to this music—and faced the facts. Above all, the facts of growing: its steady, stately, carefully grained tempo.

♩

Mud and scum are not exclusive to nature alone, but are also virulent members of the soul brigade. Their tones can be harsh and furious, but more often they speak in grey monotones of despair, alienation, and emptiness. "A flat calm, great mirror of my despair," writes Baudelaire, supreme investigator of anomie and morbid addiction. Nor can one be surprised any longer by the inevitable symbiosis connecting alienation to its vengeful counterpart, violent wrath.

In his exquisite and gripping study of the poetic process, *The Bow and the Lyre*, Octavio Paz outlines his therapy for resisting modern man's accelerating flight from the Garden of Eden into a world made pallid and plastic by technological glut. The remedy is poetry, of course, poetry as fact and as metaphor to repair the augmenting gulf between man and his surroundings, man and his being. There are two necessary steps: first, a profound contemplation of nature until we are in tune with its rhythms, can hear and articulate them, can overcome our instinctive fear of alien forces; and then, an essential recovery of that nothingness which precedes being, that state of benign uncertainty which is the original but corrupted source for the bastardized progeny which currently afflict us: futility, anxiety, boredom.

Therefore, to study what Nietzsche calls "the incomparable vivacity of life," and to fashion statements and artifacts of appreciation; to accept bravely the condition of nothingness as the inalterable premise of existence; and to construct a being which can incorporate such tenuous roots and beginnings: these are the facts and their appropriate responses, according to Paz.

¿

What has all this to do with musical performance and piano playing?

In response to the indifference and inaccessibility of the natural world, Paz offers a delectable, penetrating haiku from the pen of the Japanese poet Buson.

before the white chrysanthemums
the scissors hesitate
for an instant

The commentary of Paz follows:

> *That instant reveals the unity of being. All is still and*
> *all is in motion. Death is not a thing apart: it is, in an*
> *inexpressible way, life. The revelation of our nothingness*
> *leads us to the creation of being. Thrown into the nothing,*
> *man creates himself in the face of it.*
>
> *The poetic experience is a revelation of our original*
> *condition. And that revelation is always resolved into a*
> *creation: the creation of our selves. The revelation does not*
> *uncover something external, which was there, alien, but*
> *rather the act of uncovering involves the creation of that*
> *which is going to be uncovered: our own being.*

When we play music we describe and echo the tableau
of natural forms, their shapes and arrangements, as uncov-
ered by the composer's imagination, which yet must be
filtered through our own. There is no other way. And in
acknowledging this tableau, this revelation, we must "hesitate," we must doubt, as the composer doubted, for no
valid creation can issue unscarred by doubt, by that vast
flux of wonder which precedes the construction of being.

When we play, this gentle, uneasy, fluctuating, nameless,
stark condition of wonder infiltrates the tone and diction
of every tone; without it no fake bluster of certitude, no
glib assurance of set formulas can compensate or cover up
the existential void. This doubt, born in fear and trembling,
is not a liability; it is a sign of a contemplative wisdom
which is unafraid to admit fear into its poetic construct,
and which is the indispensable prelude to conviction and
faith.

THE TEXT

Musical scores are like maps, whose signposts, roads, connections, detours become the blueprint for musical forms, and as well the forums for blue notes imprinted onto the senses. Blue notes, grey notes, notes which are granitic or bituminous, luminous or silky, cavernous or vexing, leafy or redolent—thus the musical imagination projects the features of a landscape onto the map of the score. For the pianist, for whom the written notes are tangibly black and white, carbon and oxygen, the task of portraying the full landscape is infinitely difficult, the rewards infinitely precious.

𝄽

The score is fixed, and its instructions are an infallible, inviolable canon. Interpretation is thereby limited, even condemned to the integers and integrations posed by the score, an ever-demanding priest of Authority. Stray from its boundaries and you are branded heretic, infidel, or genius. Nevertheless, to fixate on the surface of the score is to cheat, cheating life, cheating the bewildering mixture of continuity and contingency which is the nature of life and the charm of music.

𝄽

The urtext is the holy and primordial code. Of what? Of an oracle who speaks in graphic riddles, of a style once familiar and forever attenuated, of the traceries of an inspiration as brilliant and ephemeral as a meteor. Or perhaps the vestiges of a forgotten god, or even the detritus of an exotic or extinct beast—as in the exquisite dung patterns of a dinosaur or those of a more friendly, furry species. Perhaps this is the basis for such mystical evocations as the Koala Lump Ur, secret cipher of the learned. Whichever, it commands our attention.

𝄽

Do you particularly admire the lemon groves? Or do you prefer almond trees, modestly dressed in pink flowers, or the swarthy, supple limbs of olive trees, or cypress or eucalyptus, or birch, banyan, baobab, or perhaps the quiet reticence of briar? There is a dark and arid story going around, a grave, self-fulfilling theory which claims that music is about—and only about—music: a system of independent symbols constituting an alternate lifestyle exclusive of life and its list of lifestyles. Alas, tell that to the Australian aboriginals Bruce Chatwin has described in *The Songlines*. Tell that to the pianist who has played "Bruyères" by Debussy.

♩

Musical performance tends to become the province of charlatans, countesses, and accountants. There are generally two modes of expression available to interpreters, a tender lyricism intended to reconstitute the myths of some ancien régime; and the flashy fusillades delivered by the Virtuosi di Bomba. The audience, capable of distinguishing black from white, is enchanted. The cognoscenti, capable of distinguishing cognac from cola, is equally satisfied. Only one condition must be met: all performances must be executed with a cosmetic precision worthy of a new Lexus.

♩

One is either a bird or a horse or a muffin. If the lyrical dreamers are birds and the artillery experts are horses, then who are the muffins? Alas, the muffins do not survive well in this grim and grueling profession. More prevalent, instead, are the worthy Gothic stonemasons. True artisans, they chisel out their grey stones of devotion with seemingly monastic purity. Through them we can conjure up the liturgical origins of music. Nor can one blame them if the troubadour and the minstrel, who sing of bluebirds and wild horses, are missing. Better half a loaf than none, though the flour is not the bread.

♩

If there is such a thing as a blue note, could there not also be green notes and mauve notes? Notes can be just notes, of course, devoid of shadow or color, therefore hardly noteworthy. Something like batter partitioned in a cookie mold—inedible and unedifying. Notes that do not denote or connote belong only to factories, and can never appeal to the olfactories of the Muse and her followers. What makes the difference, then? It is when the notes couple, swoon, and despair in mutual attraction or repulsion, when they embellish each other by their common and alien scents, until there are more colors and more fragrances than names to describe them. But the poor, unshelled eunuch notes are forever confined to a grainy monotone.

♭

The piece is: itself, its genes, its schemes; its means, its network, its print, its blueprint, its fingerprint. It stands for nothing, but it stands—like a sequoia, like the Watts Towers. It survives to the degree that its motivic cells, whether articulated through pitch or rhythm, color or dynamics, are integrated and elaborated, yet exogamous: sufficiently contrasting to create tension, mystery, progeny. It is an organism whose features are interconnected by multiple filaments, as though when a centipede moves one leg, a spectrum of harmonized responses resonates, however subtly, in the remaining ninety-nine. By this standard of the interdependence, fluency, and complexity of its parts, the formal validity of the piece will be measured.

♭

The piece is: a structure, a specimen, an organization of tones cannily wrought to self-sufficiency. All these, but something else: its shadow, its radiance, its aura, its meaning. The piece is, but inevitably, the piece says. What? What does it say, what does it mean? What seeds of doubt, or dream, or desire does it sow? For it is helpless to avoid these intimations, these confessions. Whether Boulez or Bach, the geometry of tones can never shed the legacy of musical ancestors, of musical language itself forever imprinted with the primal cri de coeur and all its rivers of symbolism. It was not an idle dispensation of God that made it happen; it was to find a bridge to that God, to lament and to celebrate this bewildering message.

ф

By what criteria, then, does the interpretation of this message proceed? How shall we portray the particular piece, discover its characteristics of meaning and aura, decide whether it is blue or bellicose? And ultimately, which shade of blue, which stride, which steed, which perspective of land and luminary? Can the answer be researched, or is the solution entirely fortuitous? Is there a process, a sequence, a formula for deciphering such ephemeral and enigmatic yet potent clues?

The short answer is no. Meaning is a perpetual fiction which eludes us progressively as we come closer. The long answer, long in preparation, is yes. A qualified yes, of course, but available to the degree that we can match evanescence with wary grace and imagination.

ф

Meanings are decimated. As the veneer of "progress" eroded, humanity confronted its basic emotions without the leavening of its dying myths. So that greed, venality, anxiety, hatred, and fear became the currency of the soul; only competition provided relief, a sense of purpose and urgency. If not through war, then through a variety of consumer addictions, whether commodities, hallucinogens, or the stuff of gracious living. As words became tools and things became toys, art was stripped of its twin rhetoric, nobility and contemplative wonder. Therefore so much of modern music seems relatively "purposeless." It is and it must be, to retain its dignity, to say no to manipulation and fatuous lies.

ф

The professions of piano, of music, and of the music business are populated by a variety of types and the strata they represent, ranging from front-line workers to adjutants to adjudicators to experts to professors to informed consumers, all of whom thrive on the sanctity of their own opinions. For the nature of musical language, sufficiently nebulous to resist verifiable fact or theory, invites wistful or acid or shallow prejudices posing as august wisdom. The arenas for such display of the most characteristic of all human gifts, rationalization, are endless: the newspaper, the professional journal, the boardroom, the audition, the studio, the competition, the concert hall. Everybody is an expert, yet curiously they all share similar opinions.

𝄐

As they say, the romance is over. The jargon of cynicism, lament, pseudo-analysis, and psychoanalysis is rife, while the litanies of joy are reduced to sentimental postcards and the silent wonders of nature's scroll. Music, most immune from the sophistry of matter, must yet defend its license to be. To be nothing but a tissue of dreams, epiphanies, and ideals. Yet without the hearth of a reasonable and soaring language, music becomes but a code for the initiated and a commodity for the many. For the young practitioner it becomes a ladder to respectability, a career option, an exercise in pleasing the warlords and gourmands of the profession. Genuine self-awareness, self-examination, even self-esteem are surreptitiously abandoned in the absence of a coherent scheme of thought, and of a mythology of great deeds and dreams.

𝄐

My student lamented that an art critic in discussing Chagall had dismissed him as nought but a poet, as though lacking in compositional structure and solidity. Thus poetic sensibility in itself was insufficient, for fantasy cannot sustain itself without the grammar of architectural space. The implied prejudice of such a comment concerns the very nature of form. Classical forms, geometrically divided into balanced areas and planes, are considered more legitimate than free-flowing forms wanting in sharp boundaries, right angles, and dialectics.

Nevertheless, Debussy is supposed to have remarked (snidely) about Beethoven development sections, "Here is where the mathematics begin." It turns out finally that nature, in its infinite wisdom, is equally prolific in forms that meander or reproduce by fractals. Arithmetic is only one of its charms.

♩

The concept of "musicality" is the first refuge of the musical patriot. It is typically employed to describe a kind of amorphous singsong which swaddles the music with aimlessly undulating contours, suggesting a sweet and obedient nature. It is agreeable enough, but often an impediment to a more valid musical rhetoric. For true pathos demands more than a sympathetic nature; it also requires accent, tension, dislocation, turbulence, or their antithesis, dead calm.

♩

What we call "musical" has only one component of valid meaning: its converse, unmusical. Indeed, it is an awful charge to make, but here and there such characters do exist, a few disjointed souls who can reasonably be labeled unmusical. They usually come in either of two categories, politicians or musical experts, sharing the same cynicism, complacency, and rigid lust for clichés. Fortunately there are exceptions, such as the former governor of Louisiana.

♩

Musical playing, which would appear to be so natural and unforced, as capacious as a corn muffin, as cheerful as popcorn, is in fact full of makeup and make-believe. It is like the face of a modern starlet, anonymous and smooth as a plastic button, graded and beveled by the appropriate creams, surgeons, and camera angles. It is playing which is designed to please, never to challenge or offend. It represents the consensus character of beauty, but it is far from the beauty of character. It is like the face of a fashion model compared to the face of Bette Davis.

ǫ

That circuitous winding up and down the line which echoes the platitudes of genteel expression may be symptomatic of musical playing at its most tepid and self-satisfied. By an odd though audible illusion, however, there is a subversive neighbor to this idiom which superficially resembles it, yet is intensely different and compelling. For the greatest performers have a quality in their diction and psychology which occasionally will muse on the purely speculative and enigmatic, and which falls into a style that may fairly be described as digressive or meandering—the meandering of streams (of consciousness) and of poetic flights. In this authentic way the search goes on, nor can prior formulas shape it.

ǫ

Music is a series of de-forming questions and conforming answers. The answers are less urgent, in that they tend to reinforce the will to glory, mastery, and contentment. They are the necessary bromides and homilies which even the greatest composers affirm. But the *questions*, which staple the pain of living to the quest for meaning and redemption, are ultimately the agents which reveal and penetrate, and which by contrast make the cadence seem but a courtesy, a curtsy.

ǫ

The opening theme of Beethoven's first piano sonata announces the composer's immediate, forceful intentions, and, as well, his ultimate moral philosophy. The phrase begins with a declaration of territory, which is progressively compressed and concentrated until it becomes but a motto, a stamp of authority. At that point it breaks down and collapses under the weight of its own zeal. The dictates of imperialism, of absolutism of any kind are always constrained by the forces of biology, of divergence and new growth.

ᕤ

Certain themes from certain pieces have a quality so legendary and iconic that we cannot believe they are the product of human toil. I am not referring to examples such as "White Christmas" or the "Ode to Joy," propagated through so many levels of exploitation that they have lost their pedigree and become cultural junk bonds, but rather more obscure instances—for example, the principal theme from the second movement of Schumann's Piano Quintet. The maddening, haunting nature of this theme, so uncannily poised between resignation and resistance, despair and defiance, seems embedded in the stones, a tablet left by some merciless angel who wills us to command our grief. The eloquence is beyond human intervention. Uniting deliverance and the grave, it defies the laws of both gravity and causality.

ᕤ

A student working on Scriabin's sixth piano sonata was disturbed when one of her colleagues dismissed Scriabin as but a mystic. To cheer her up I told her the story of the Dalai Lama, who, upon visiting New York City, asked the hot-dog vendor to "make me one with everything." Mysticism can be quite embracing; nor is it a sign of intellectual deficiency. Of course, contrasted to the practice of Mozart and friends, whose forms sustain a variety of ideas in enlightened conversation, the univocal appeal of Scriabin and his reliance upon a single chord as repository for motivic invention may seem parochial and limited. But this reaction is partly a function of our eye prejudice, the eye that arranges and regulates space. If we use our ears, however, a lexicon of tone color will emerge from Scriabin which creates another and vivid kind of counterpoint, a counterpoint of colors no less differentiated because they are invisible.

𝒬

The triad of ethical imperatives which predominate in musical society promotes the ideals of the "simple" and the "natural," supporting the arch concept of the "musical." All three, unfortunately, are often but rationalizations for a lack of vigor and imagination. What is genuinely imaginative is mostly misunderstood and dismissed by resort to the following terms of non-endearment: eccentric, meretricious, artificial, intellectual (!), willful, weird, and the like. The comfortable, two-dimensional, pedantic mind is disturbed by creative and complex imagery. That is why it despises contemporary classical music.

𝒬

Shakespeare bemoaned "simple truth called simplicity." Simple truth may exist, but it is simply the void at the center of cutting and contradictory truths. It is a wisdom based upon the recognition of fallibility and separate claims, far from doctrines of the infallible and the ordained. It is a teleological emptiness, a denuded core of mind and sound which is beyond approval or protest, though it may honor the pieties of lullaby and folksong as poignant memory or loss. It never feeds on reductive rhymes or slogans. And when they drag out the shibboleth "Less is more," the telling rejoinder was delivered by the architect Robert Venturi: "Less is a bore."

ḁ

Art is a process of concentration. It is both the distilled essence and the commentary upon otherwise mundane activities and reflections. Musical notes must be charged, must gather more than one and the surface meaning, must reveal audible and "inaudible" connections to other notes, patterns, and meanings, either by way of affinity or contrast. As Coleridge defined it, the special nature of the poetic imagination lies in its ability to juxtapose and ally two otherwise unrelated, discrete images. The key to the musical imagination is a similar capacity to derive multiple meanings from a group of notes, or even single notes, which can plausibly be testimonies of either doubt or cheer, chance or affirmation.

ḁ

When the poet Constantine Cavafy chose to proscribe all metaphor from his writing, a principle of discipline and candor was invoked. In this way he provided compelling evidence for the theory that a work of art expresses itself as a balance sheet pitting the spoken against the unspoken. The same potential is available when we play our notes. They may bleed, but the blood is stanched; they may suggest, but they are stilled; they may sing, but they are hushed: a stoic endurance prevails. Yet if we choose Cavafy's route of non-discursiveness, of that tableau of indiscriminate sensation to be purged and crystallized by incisive language, it should be as a choice from the cauldron of variables, never casual nor expedient.

ḁ

Of all the charming conceits propounded by the defenders of the good and the musical, the most innocuous, yet perhaps noxious, is the ideal of the "natural." As though nature were a compound of Plato and PlaySkool, orderly mannequins agreeably deployed with set palm trees rippling in the background. However, if the "natural" were truly a derivative of nature, then musical performance would be quite different. It would express the turbulent, the menacing, and a beauty as voluptuous and volatile as in the poetry of Gerard Manley Hopkins. The better part of what is called natural is the effortless: physical and musical friction ameliorated by elegant coordination. The worse part is an accommodating flow which ceases to be either statement or substance, but is merely spin.

𝆕

Before musicality there is musicianship. After musicality there is musicianship. Musicality is typically the crayon version of a diluted musicianship, aware of the forest and the silhouette but untutored in the trees, wildlife, and chemistry. Musicianship is in the quartermaster's corps of notational signs and their expressive correlations. It contains a script of limited components with limitless implications; nor is there any simple, natural, or musical way of deciphering this code. There is only an artistic way—of identifying the ingredients and making difficult choices. It is a radical, complex, and dutiful process.

𝆕

The gliding and soaring prowess of birds is a function of their intimate relationship with the wind. They gain momentum and direction from the wind by navigating its currents. If the subject of musical phrasing, by itself, were a staple course in the conservatory curriculum, then ornithology and wind mechanics would be essential features. The boxed, frigid phrasings of many performances in the marketplace can be explained as a slighting of the world as atmosphere, as current, as turbulence—i.e., the dynamics of flow and its infinite variables.

⟨⟩

All musical phrases have a beginning, a middle, an end. Of course some of them seem oddly undomesticated, apparently beginning in the middle and ending where they should begin. That is, they may begin with an unbridled energy or finish in ways more searching than placid. The variables that determine the destiny of the phrase—be they functions of line, rhythm, harmony, counterpoint—do not always behave as anticipated. They do not always conform to the design of the cherished Roman arch, bereft of swerving, branching, or unwanted ivy. Phrases contain seeds of growth, development, and destruction; their tendency to soaring parabolas is sometimes affected by poignant contingencies and detours.

The capacity to differentiate among the various lines and features of the phrase is called, quaintly, voicing. Its implications are profound: to hear, respect, and fulfill the meanings, however subliminal, of the other voices. The reason that we often misunderstand Schumann lies in our failure to read his phrases as havens for shadowy colonies of inner voices intimating irony, resistance, or bemusement.

⟨⟩

When the variables of a dynamic system are sufficiently complex and volatile, their observation and study has been appropriated by a relatively new branch of mathematical physics identified under the rubric of chaos theory. The name itself betrays, with appropriate wit and irony, the human prejudice against capricious, unregenerate variables. For if the phenomena cannot be reduced to the prevailing credo or model, they are per se unruly and intractable: chaotic.

Dear scientists, welcome to the world of musical phrases and structures.

⟨⟩

In chaos theory, two significant factors are the concept of "initial starting conditions," as derived from the work of the French mathematician Jules-Henri Poincaré; and the "butterfly effect," as propounded by the M.I.T. scientist Edward Lorenz. Both factors are vital and implicit to the understanding of musical phrases and forms.

The successful interpretation of any work of art depends upon the recognition of those germinal elements which proliferate in both recurrent and transformed shapes throughout the work. The connections, however overt or covert, between the basic cells and their varieties of elaboration are of ultimate strategic importance. Not unexpectedly, these connections do not always reside on the surface of the music.

The butterfly effect (so designated by the notion that a butterfly shaking its wings over Honolulu may eventually alter the weather pattern over Pittsburgh) has clear musical analogues. One presumably obscure note, raised from dormancy or disuse, may cast a light (or shadow) which can alter, even reverse the predictable outcome of a phrase. Since the urge of music is constantly to evolve and transform, such notes and signs of latent change or subversion are essential ingredients of the process.

℘

Painting consists substantially of a dialogue between objects and their environment. The dialogue is intense, and it acts as a solution and context necessary to establish the character and isolation of the separate constituents. Thus the Mona Lisa would become an idiot cartoon if robbed of the surrounding planes of landscape, while the grain stacks of Monet are yet repositories and crucibles for the light and atmosphere which feed and are fed by them. In a musical phrase the notes are validated by the timings between them, and by the dynamic gradations which reflect these timings. The telling guide is nature, so that the timings correspond to atmospheric motion, to the chemistry of light and wind which provides a diagram for the infinite contours of phrasing. The phrase must float, must circulate freely, akin to Leon Fleisher's apt counsel and image of "antigravity." The timings are vital to the design of the phrase, inflecting the syntax with durations both regular and irregular. The wind, in its fabled repertoire of zephyr to storm, is the wisest teacher, and yet we remember that apparent stillness is one of its most profound lessons.

♩

For the spinning out of phrases according to the laws of aerodynamics and levitation, two of the most gifted members of the windhover clan are the classical oboist Heinz Holliger and the jazz saxophonist Stan Getz. Ironically, the arching twists of Holliger's lines seem the more jazzy and feverish, while the parabolas of Getz are more classical and serene. Both respond to the living moment of sound, the wayward fallout of breath and frequency, the eternal fraction of random over design. Like arabesques of smoke curling into the light, the phrase aspires, a permanent elegy to impermanence.

♩

My teacher, Mr. Steuermann, once premised a theory accounting for the universal hunger for music upon an observation made by Nietzsche, to the effect that the ear is the organ of fear. Thus music became necessary to assuage the anxiety inherent to the hearing faculty, and to console and reassure against all demons actual or imaginary. It is not a great leap backward to speculate that prehistoric man, who could identify his adversaries in the daytime, could only distinguish by ears alone their rattlings, cries, grunts, slitherings at night. In fact, the anthropologists have so described the conditions of primitive nocturnal life on the savannas of Africa.

Thus, charmed music evolves to become the antidote to our nightmares, the accompaniment to our daydreams, the elixir that sustains faith.

♀

The musical commentary of Donald Tovey (1875–1940) is distinguished by a wide-ranging style combining multiple and contrasting perspectives, the diversity of which is relatively uncommon to contemporary music studies and criticism. Alongside copious structural analyses of a particular work, Tovey unashamedly offers compelling insights into the specific psychological, expressive, and dramatic details of the piece, using an approach which renders wholly congruent both the technical and poetic discussions of music.

Contemporary scholars and critics are usually far more reluctant to offer such comprehensive insights. The philosophy of art as self-referential, as meaningful only in terms of its internal signs and associations, has secured a substantial hold on the cadre of most influential scholars and authorities. On the other hand, biographical analysis has yielded to a hemorrhaging tendency to psychoanalyze or deconstruct the artist. From this vantage point the music is perceived as the issue of dynamic distempers and Freudian complexes. The genesis of each composition is identified by tracking the composer's manic-depressive surges and failed love affairs.

The vision of music as an adventurous and poetic eye on the universe is squeezed by the inroads of two violently opposed critical attitudes: dry analysis and psychological banter.

𝆕

Paradoxically, some critics, in their occasional polemics, appear to welcome an interpretive approach more receptive to risk and spontaneity than the prevailing norm might encourage. This is especially true of that small group of commentators who distinguish themselves by echoing Ezra Pound's theory of criticism, wherein "enthusiasm" itself is the primary responsibility. Unfortunately the matrix of conditions affecting the music profession, from deadlines to compressed available space, from fashionably pedantic analysis to axioms of marketability, from the limited rehearsal time of conductors to the ungenerous, uptight psyche of the recording muse, presents critics with a basic set of musical options inhospitable to certain distinctions of interpretation, often labeled as deviant.

For there is no discourse in current use to apprehend these distinctions. The style constraints of both performance and its forms of description are so fixed that fantasy itself is met with a condemning reflex, and is usually decried by summoning up the epithets "sentimental" or "artificial," along with their respective progeny. Needless to say, I am not referring here to those sympathetic amateurs employed by smaller newspapers who may indiscriminately indulge their heart.

𝆕

There is one principle which is perpetual, autonomous, unblinking, and uncompromising and must be honored at all times: the law of the score. The score is the boss to whom we must be eternally loyal and faithful.

But this boss is not stern. He is full of ginger and play, and of the conversation of ideas. When we follow him most faithfully we are drawn into a symposium both grand and delightful, but hostile to abbreviated slogans. Nor does he want a generic performance representative of a certain (alleged) style. Instead, he wants to be a very special individual whose every sound and inflection should be cherished, both singular and grouped, concrete and visionary.

When my teacher sat next to Schoenberg at the premiere of the *Gurrelieder*, the composer turned to him in the middle of some huge climax and asked urgently, "Can you hear the *pizzicati* in the celli?!"

When we follow the score, in fact and in spirit, we arrive at the most arresting and novel of interpretations.

ò

The path of so-called style and the path of the score do not always overlap. Style is an approximation, a retrospective noose which would reconcile (and domesticate) composers and scores no more companionable in spirit than the opposing wings of the Democratic Party. Such vague guidelines, ossified by habit, operate most effectively when applied to inferior and conventional music. The style is but the convention, which interesting and memorable music will allude to, wink at, and pass by on the road to adventure.

Scores are active, virulent, prophetic things which do not rest well behind glass nor exude simple nostalgia when pressed like the flowers of first love. Scores look back, look ahead, and yet dance in the streets of here and now. They are brusque, brooding, feisty, mysterious, subtle, disarming, and incorrigible. They speak in a thousand tongues, ancient and unborn, and only the combined efforts of an archaeologist, a seer, and a Sancho Panza can hope to make sense of them.

As performers, critics, teachers, students, and scholars, we must not mistake the safe haven of style for the daring maneuvers of the vessel.

℺

Behind every work of art or its execution, there exists a Platonic blueprint, unshakable and inevitable, which acts as a source of fixed information. In music, such factors as harmonic functions, formal relationships—in particular, rhythmic equivalencies and conversions—are natural constituents of this map, whose laws operate in every domain of the literature.

And yet even this prime set is victim to the subversions of life and its idioms. Exhibit A of imperial authority, the sanctity of rhythmic durations, is yet vulnerable to the predations, good and bad, of expressive need or fancy. When Schnabel said that the sixteenth passages in Mozart were simply fast melodies, it was not an invitation to rhythmic anarchy, rather a suggestion that the interests of shape and phrasing may modify in subtle ways, as gravitation bends light, the intrinsic dictatorship of rhythm.

All musical categories are malleable in the quest for expressive truth, some more and some less. As listeners we should not acquiesce to models of conformity, but take pleasure, spiced with surprise, over new and revealing alignments.

℺

Baudelaire said that in everything beautiful there is something strange. Whether that means something unfamiliar or something "weird" is immaterial, for either definition is appropriate to the spirit of performance. Any confinement of the scores by homogenous conventions of style, technical security, or the sloth of fake tradition is bad for the patient.

If one listens to the recording by Charles Panzéra and Alfred Cortot of the Schumann *Dichterliebe*, one hears the music illuminated by an insight which catches deftly the crackling and eternal dynamic that binds detail to whole, that *banishes* the "details" as distinct from the whole. The performance forces the mind to stare for one spellbound, prescient, infinite moment through some peephole of doom, grace, or jollies while yet immersed in the cyclical vision. The compound of pain and grandeur which sustains the music is threaded with distracting dangers and comforting vows. The whole is both more and less than the sum of the parts. Concrete time and indivisible timelessness coexist in wary and tender embrace.

𝄞

The contradictory, consuming, contested relationship between detail and whole, event and eventuality, breathes fire and wisdom into every great work of art. A great performance should examine this contest at every level. Nothing is more lame than the attitude that the music should be left alone, should "speak for itself," should come out neat and sleek as a newborn schooner minus barnacles, seaweed, and other varieties of scabrous organisms. From this confined angle, the tidal current moves in one direction only, straight ahead; correspondingly, our spine is fused, the senses are blinkered, and all travail is evicted from travel.

The biology of music is betrayed by such a one-ended telescope, through which one sees the image of a star but not its chemistry, turbulence, or neighbors. The modern temperament, however, deluged with bits, data, software, and graphics, is desperate to organize, streamline, weed out the messy incursions of life butting in. Music then becomes a rest home, a bastion of predictability, order, and retirement.

𝄞

When one explores a composition, two tenets must govern the investigation: to find the spirit and vision of the piece; to identify the stations and locales of its odyssey. One must experience it from both perspectives, immediate and distant. Definitions of the overall spirit should remain suitably vague (making room for future discovery) until the journey proceeds in earnest. Thus the stations get the immediate attention, each one a locus of action and image, and whose quality, significance, and destiny are to be hotly debated.

What does this mean? What does that say? Name it; provide a meaning, a face, a haunt, a ground; a role, a dream, a fate, and its part of the plot. Which part? Obedient, conforming, deforming, derailing, didactic, intactful, slender, slanderous, tame, or tepid? No, never tepid, however quiescent. Quiet has a pulse too.

♩

Now comes the impossible job requiring the patience of Job: the proof by faith alone that notes and chords, motives and phrases have distinct, decipherable names, colors, and auras, representing images of precise description and coordinates. The working musician in the pits, in the mines, laying fortifications or defending them, knows in the tummy of his heart that every note has such a name, from Ulalume to daisy to mulch.

Of course, it is amply self-evident that one man's Desi is another man's Lucy; therefore no tone can be permanently endowed with a single indisputable name. Which is why they make chocolate and vanilla. But given your right to call it as you hear it, you have no right, as a musician or sensate being, *not* to call it, or ignore or dismiss it as but pretty scrollwork on the column supporting the throne of the Maker.

Only the Maker shall be nameless, and all Its angels and granules of sand shall have distinct and colorful names.

𝆕

The child shall take the dowsing rod, walk around and scratch his head until he finds the magic spot which guards the hidden well, then name and describe that place by its rightful endowment of properties. The name may be conditional; the act of naming is unconditional. The name may be obsolete the day after, but it should conjure up some trace, glimpse, memory of the spot as token of greeting and acknowledgment.

The scene shifts. Can one imagine, for example, Schoenberg or Rachmaninoff composing away and all the while giving bright, quirky names to their delectable spots? Not really (but who knows?). And if not, it is because their tones have been so crossed and fertilized by resolute will through so many stages of challenging voices from other languages and planets that the exercise has become reflexive. And the meaning of things so intense that gentle Music is required to elegize the gory remains, keeping private what is unmentionable but not unnamable.

𝆕

The process of naming things takes place in the laboratory of the imagination. There are two stages in this process.

The child (ourselves) should know the name of every bird, tree, species of flora and fauna within the vicinity of 12,500 miles in any direction. Then add on the names of the astronomical bodies, and bodies of literature, painting, sculpture, architecture, music, plus a few other odd million facts, even the names of famous horses. Bucephalus—now that's a name, a name to be savored and saved for the right delectable spot in the music. Or Whirlaway! Fantastic, heart-palpitating, galvanizing our wildest dreams and fairy tales. Or Seabiscuit!! What name in the history of the universe can rival the gracious moniker of this heroic thoroughbred? Whose very name bounds and balms with matching brilliance?

Identifying the total cast of characters is job number one.

ꝗ

Gorging on names is the appetizer. Each trifle or truffle is lovingly evoked and laid out on the wooden block for ceremonial investiture. Then begins the delicate exercise of comparing one thing to another by the modes, chemistries, colors, properties of each, matching them by any thread available. This is the game of transitions and metaphors, and, children ourselves, we must practice it assiduously. Everything belongs in some way to everything else, a chain of being whether being or inanimate. Some matches are made in heaven, some in hell, some in limbo. Practice and genius do better in their matchmaking.

A certain Renaissance painter observed that when he visited the veterans' hospitals he would invariably notice the spittle on the walls of the wards lodging tubercular patients. In the patterns of that spittle he could see the possibilities for great paintings.

To the practiced eye, everything may explode with meaning.

ꝗ

My teacher mentioned to me that Alban Berg once complained to Schoenberg, his teacher, that Liszt's transformation of the lyrical theme from his Second Piano Concerto into a rowdy march was rather, if I may paraphrase, déclassé. As relayed to me, Schoenberg replied somewhat scornfully, Why not? The appropriateness of certain associations and metaphors is largely a matter of taste, temperament, and training. But some juxtapositions, if not legally invalid, should be exiled to the isle of no-man.

When Rolaids uses the Fifth Symphony to promote ant-acids, one is prone to a big tummy ache (and use of the product). When a financial institution uses Beethoven's *Choral Fantasy*, the most innocent and disinterested of cre-ations, to sell dreams of Mammon, the institution is witless and without redeemable value. When the rock vamp dan-gles with equal aplomb a crucifix and the Pepsi-Cola logo, only Lavoris and lobotomy will do.

̣ǫ

If music be the art to which all other arts aspire, if its language be self-contained and insulated from verbal or log-ical confusions, if it unfolds as a cinema of inmost feelings, what difference does the environment, physical and intel-lectual, make for its study?

And yet, if the nonverbal language of music makes it purely symbolic, symbolic of what? If music is self-contained, what is the container? If music is about vague and nameless emotions, what differentiates the spiritual quality of one piece from another?

Music is about something. Its sources are discoverable, its meanings are discernible. It possesses an unusual power derived from its placement at both ends of the verbal scale: as primordial, embryonic hothouse of seething or evanes-cent image; as temple of distilled thought. But this polarity only thickens the plot, making the nature of the musical image more volatile or Delphic, but not less real or grasp-able, not less indebted to the tangent and tangible land-scape which it devours and extols.

̣ǫ

Rubato is not a maraschino cherry perched on top of a scoop of vanilla ice cream, providing a shot of exotic color to otherwise bland fare. You cannot graft a spitcurl of per-sonality onto a blank, impassive forehead. *Rubato* is a way and *category* of musical life, whether pronounced or subtle, conspicuous or undetectable. It is always there, built into patterns as mechanical as Alberti basses and investing the most fundamentalist rhythms with profiles of courage, tenderness, or elegance.

No human being can, or even should, produce durations of absolute equivalence. One should be thoroughly trained, as a matter of course, in the opposite poles of metronomic invariability and rhetorical freedom. Certainly the quality of evenness is desirable and necessary, if only as a foil to expressive freedom. But absolute evenness is an illusion, while the character of *consistency* is in fact but the product of subtle adjustments. For if the subdivided units of the figuration were mathematically equivalent, the effect would be tedium, not consistency.

𝄽

Mozart's advice to pianists—the left hand in strict time, the right hand *rubato*—is still and permanently appropriate. Inherent to any musical conception is the fated and critical divergence between the respective interests of linear time and "spatial" time. For time not only moves inexorably forward, as the underlying grid to our personal chronicle, but is manipulated by our psychic needs and natures into various images of timelessness and timeliness. Transient moments suddenly expand, visions of infinity intervene, notes and phrases become outlets of fantasy, escape, recollection, or omen. The music travels on two planes, chronological time and psychological time. Both planes are essential and must be abundantly represented. The preponderance of *rubato* activity, lavish or discreet, occurs in the psychological plane, the right hand in Mozart's prescription. But even the agent of linear time, the left hand, must argue its case by delineations which can only approximate perfect equivalency.

The nature of consistency should be thoroughly grasped,

but to execute its relentless mission requires slight variations of timing as well as touch.

♀

When John Locke divided the nature of objects into primary and secondary properties, art was done an unwitting slight. For that aspect which in large part is the province of art, the shape and color and feel of an object as experienced by the senses, was deemed secondary, while primary status was conferred upon the physics and chemistry of the object.

But then it turned out that the same chaos, uncertainty, and asymmetry functional to the senses were also relevant to the speculations of science. The straight lines and right angles which are anathema to our perception of nature are equally invalid in the living, non-Euclidean science. Space itself is intrinsically curved.

Evenness, or equivalence, as a Platonic archetype is an inevitable warlord of our imagination. But making its message clear and forceful demands, nevertheless, a particular formula of recurring units minutely tilting one way or another. For pure evenness is only a state of mind reflecting a certain monotony or aggressiveness. But forceful consistency will always betray a slight limp or prejudice.

♀

Music is a revolt against Time—time as the chronicle of equal moments and of mortal spans. Music aims for transcendence, for the gathering of rosebuds and the rendezvous with eternity. Music turns the mundane moment into a bower of infinite pleasure and redemptive understanding, assembling its flowing moments into orbits of curved and complex time. Music dispels the fear of mortality and the need for rigid and permanent identities. Music rejects the nine-to-five schedule, the hunger for cash, the encroachments and limits of crass appetite. Music is a cake which grows as you eat it, which has seven layers and seven more for each layer.

Paradoxically, apparently equivalent and imperturbable metric units must exist within music against which to measure the scope of the adventure and trace the parabola of the flight. Paradoxically, these metric units have an inner life of their own which reproduces them faithfully but not mechanically.

♩

The manner of executing the rhythmic values of linear time (and its relentless claims in behalf of "reality") is a matter of much debate and inspiration. The simplest accompaniment in Mozart or Schubert, compounded of innocuous figurations in the public domain, requires a special sensitivity to deal with its several dimensions. First, it must create a sustaining harmonic environment; second, it must provide contrapuntal activity, however embryonic or modest, which both supports and contrasts the melodic line; third, it must hold fast to its job as timepiece against the reveries and exclamations of the main voice. The accompaniment then nourishes, blends, contrasts, counters the rhetorical escapades of the melody.

The integration of these separate duties of the accompaniment cannot be fused into a zombie-like pulse which ignores the variety of its functions. Even the timpani in its most methodical assignment must exude the sweat, the will of its psychic destiny; therefore, its part must be conditioned by its role in the overall drama.

♩

An unconditionally even pulse is an abstract ideal which must be acknowledged, even sought, but can never be realized except as illusion. Yet the illusion of a gentle or pounding pulse is an essential constituent of the dramatic interplay, and producing it requires a canny appreciation of its precise character in relation to the whole. Nevertheless, the concept (and prospect) of absolute rhythmic equivalence is inherently undermined by the permanent "tragedy" of metric organization. For there always is a downbeat, and there always is a weak beat; never shall these twain find a perfectly stable equilibrium. The tendency of the strong beat to impose its will and the reciprocal desire of the weak beat to resist that will create an uneasy truce which can never be reduced to a comfortable hierarchical formula. The internal tension always retains the potential for uncertainty and rebellion. The weak beats demand status, conspiring and threatening to unseat the dictatorial downbeat. This unavoidable restlessness only echoes a certain ambiguity, even treachery, native to linear time, which would guarantee continuity as it yet reminds of infirmity and transience.

Thus, even the voice which chronicles neutral reality is in some sense a victim of the stresses of *rubato*.

♩

"Everybody knows that the music goes from the dominant to the tonic," my teacher remarked, "but the question is—how does it get there?"

Reductive theories abound in music, theories which identify significant notes and progressions as the definitive agents of the musical argument. Some of these theories reduce the material to but a few strategic tones or intervals, deriving the total structure and meaning of the work from such cryptic evidence. Thus the structural features of a sonata or symphony can conceivably be distilled into paradigmatic progressions of three or four notes. The power of the composition becomes then a function of the consistency and dominance of this unifying principle.

Such approaches can be both valuable and dangerous. It is indisputable that in every art form or natural form there are architectural beams and foci which serve as scaffolding, as framework for the welter of material. The structural and aesthetic canons surrounding the unity/variety equation are a subject of eternal debate, forever pressing and enigmatic. The urge to unify, to simplify is all too human. If we can fly from Orlando to Spokane, avoiding all the miserable motels and speed traps in between, our mission is accomplished without drain or pain—except for jet lag and air "conditioning."

But suppose you want to look out the window and see the cows?

♂

Of the many withered and withering clichés which flourish in the music studio or journal, one of the more noxious is the principle of "direction"; that is, the music must always have direction, preferably and even exclusively forward direction. The power of music is portrayed as a species of propulsion, of driving energy, of its inevitable date with destiny.

What a strange form of death wish. Why must the music always go straight ahead? Does it not sometimes go sideways? or up, down, or backward in its recollective and speculative role? Of course, straight ahead can be highly addictive, as marching bands demonstrate. To latch onto a marauding shark, or a runaway freight train, or a driving tempo makes for an exciting high. Exalting such a principle of bondage over the principle of bonding ideas and characters may have attractive features, but do we want a kind of music-making which is strictly beholden to irresistible force and to the vows of unqualified allegiance?

Music indeed has tempo, has drive, has agents of motoric impulse, has long-term goals. It also has, at a minimum, a continuous soliloquy of reverie, reverence, reminiscence, and refusal, which contend in gentle or urgent dialogue with the forces that push ahead.

When charting the wind currents and the organization of a phrase, some notes will yield to, some notes will resist the momentum. Even an arrow may quiver in the wind. Certainly a heart.

𝄽

In a book which contains the writings of Edward Steuermann (*The Not Quite Innocent Bystander*, ed. Clara Steuermann, David Porter, and Gunther Schuller), my teacher mentions the "unbelievably free improvisatory interpretation" Anton Webern brought to the performance of his own music. Unfortunately the typical performances of contemporary music do not sufficiently satisfy this standard. The black eye which modern music gets is often the direct result of less than inspired, less than cultivated hearings.

That the music is serious, that its structure is complex, that its implications are profound, unsettling, and ambiguous do not necessarily make it brainy or grainy, or even unlovable. But it cannot be played in a grainy, eviscerating way; whether Chopin or Webern, music requires the same expressiveness, the same refinement of sound. Aesthetic principles of proportion, of balancing the sound are not neglected even if the sounds intended are not sweet. There are many things in life that are not sweet but demand advocacy. But even harsh intervals and chords must be polished, must be shaped into jeweled portraits without a hint of clumsiness or dry literalness.

𝄽

For the characterization of musical phrases, there are generally three levels of declamation available. The first level approximates a kind of negative rhetoric, wherein the notes are played mechanically and stiffly, without rhythmic or dynamic inflection. Although this practice happens all too frequently, such sterile diction can never be justified. The second level affords continual access to the fountain of *rubato*, whether applied discreetly or abundantly. Song itself must always have a speech component which can infuse the lyric with a personal or topical image. However balanced the structure of the line, a note of urgency must move it to and fro, must add human pathos to the ancestral chant.

The third level, especially appropriate to the characters of either piety or transfiguration, ironically shares a significant attribute (but only one!) with the first level, rhythmic "evenness." For the characterization of those phrases which are inspired by religious calm, a profound *semplice* is necessary. And for phrases in which the figurations invoke magical properties (e.g., the *Jeux d'eau* of both Liszt and Ravel), an even articulation is essential as analogue to the "geometry" of sacred nature and its forms.

Curiously, these three levels may be thought of as the unnatural, the natural, and the supernatural.

♭

Beethoven said that next to love, the best things in life were surprises. Unfortunately one hears too few surprises in most performances of Beethoven, or of other composers for that matter. The current ethic of straightforwardness and safety predisposes against risk and surprise, thereby eliminating a considerable chunk of Beethoven's game plan, a strategy which relishes dialogue, tangents, interruptions, and unexpected developments. We have sold our Faustian souls to the devils of good housekeeping.

Conversely, somebody comes along and manages to in-

flate the Three Intermezzi, op. 117, by Brahms to a duration of forty plus minutes, creating a minor sensation. The
public, anxious to be deceived by such displays of piety,
buys it and anoints the sheer novelty.

One hopes that the recent interest in Haydn piano sonatas, crammed full of willful rhetoric leading to surprise
adventures (or the teases of no exit), is a sign of coming to
terms with the forces of unbridled mischief and natural
selection. After all, straight lines are quite unnatural.

♪

". . . incapable of producing an ugly sound." Once again
these magic words show up in our favorite piano journal,
explaining the appeal of a young pianist at a recent
competition.

How misleading at best and precious at worst. Even if
the commentator means that "ugly sound" refers to sounds
ill-proportioned and imbalanced, there is still an implicit
model of "correct" balance that would inevitably censor
those sounds which are demonic, brazen, fiery, astonishing,
bold, the whole lexicon of urgency and drama. But if the
observer means by "ugly" all that is not "beautiful"—the
likely intention and pervasive outcome—once more we reduce music to puerile limits more suitable to the Pollyanna
(and false) image of ballet.

There are two unfortunate consequences of such a maud-
lin view: (1) it significantly undermines the range and function of art; (2) it trains children to be angels, depriving
them of their spirit and fire. Art indeed redeems, but it
cannot achieve that end by rejecting the tempest and fever
of life, the so-called "dark" side; for then one must throw
out everything but the last chapter of *Crime and Punishment*.
If children are going to grow into men and women, they
must acknowledge that dark side, without pretending to

be virtuous acolytes who never had a runny nose or a murderous dream.

ρ

My friend and mentor, Rudolf Kolisch, founder of the
Kolisch Quartet and one of the great musicians and violin-
ists of this century (and, as well, intimate companion and
chess partner of my teacher, Steuermann), used to say that
nobody ever wrote a Sonata for Big Tone (or even Sonata
for Beautiful Tone). To the degree that a big tone may
reinforce expressive intensity, it is of course a valid and
valuable ally. But loud only for the sake of loud, for the
sake of stirring lethargic emotions, for the sake of stirring
the bourgeoisie, for the sake of declaring the territorial imperative, for the sake of masking the absence of mind and
muse, for the sake of compensating for an abused ego,
is an attribute mostly to be condemned if publicly ap-
plauded.

For we applaud noise in many contemporary forms, and
we tune the pitch A to increasingly strident frequencies the
better to simulate brilliance. Afraid that our petitions are
not heard, we give the gods an earache as we grow deaf
from decibel overload.

ρ

Recordings have disseminated an enormous variety of
repertoire and estimable performances throughout province
and hinterland. We must be grateful for this flowering and
access, without which known and unknown compositions
would never be appreciated by caring listeners deprived of
live concerts. At the same time a standard of execution
which only artificial splicing and editing can provide has
become for some musicians and commentators the optimal
and purest way of fashioning the musical message. And for
some listeners the one-to-one relationship with the record-

ing becomes the most intimate form of dialogue with the music.

Now let us look at it from the other side. According to some observers, the increasing availability of movies on television will eventually kill off the serious film industry (certainly the quality if not the quantity). One wonders if live concerts may also be at peril because of the profusion and convenience of recordings. Hardly any young people are to be seen at live concerts. The performances are often standardized, threadbare imitations of a generic recording style—i.e., clean and uneventful. The habitual concertgoer, trained by years of dedicated interest, is now listening to pat performances which reveal the scaffolding of the work (as in the Pompidou Center in Paris), but not its vision, complexity, or scope. Varieties of black and white have captured the market, one token of which is the practice of "colorizing" old black-and-white movies, thus rendering them colorless. Such are the consequences when technology dominates the artistic impulse.

ọ

The spirit of recordings is anathema to the spirit of music. Music, both as composition and as performance, is a dissertation on the meanings of time and the timeliness of meanings. The timings and meanings of a work change from moment to moment, while the internal and external variables are in such dynamic play as to prevent the same performance from happening twice. Music is a living essay whose beginning and ending are mere formal concessions; for these boundaries are effortlessly obliterated by the music's constant presence as accompaniment to our daily activities. We live in the continuous memory of different, haunting passages flickering in and out of our consciousness.

Only mediocre or bad music can be perfectly recorded. For recordings fix and freeze, imposing a stasis incompatible with multidimensional creation. Recordings are like the photographs of a piece, pleasant views but not the piece. What is more, they are airbrushed portraits with all the pimples, scars, blemishes, surprises removed. The infallible sign of their fallacious nature is revealed in the sonically and technically pure surface which announces and sanctifies them, skewing values, favoring complexion over complexity, consigning uncertain, contingent, challenging, organic material to a lasting and harmless internment.

♩

As performers, we are stoned by the predictability and perfection of recordings, no matter how dull they may be. When we perform in the hall, this insinuating siren of absolute dependability murmurs its impervious, irresistible call, a disdainful Ondine reminding us of our nerves and apprehensions. Fantasy and spontaneity, the hallmarks of a musical sensibility, are squeezed; but if unexpectedly they should prevail, consternation would seize the audience, unaccustomed to such illuminations.

Meanwhile, no performance is possible without Big Brother, the microphone, staring coldly at you—as though it were some bloodless avatar or wingless bird. One cannot play without some enterprising soul, or station, or company wishing to can the performance for burial in some forgotten archive. Each sound, intended by muse and composer to be but sequel or prelude to other sounds, is held and imprisoned, waiting for the commissar's (record producer's) red pencil. The piece becomes a series of static poses, losing its affinity for the unknown, the legendary, the haunted, the prophetic, all the charms of transcendence and deliverance.

On the whole, we must be content with recordings, with

their glimpses of great artists of the past and of music we might otherwise never know. But we must overcome their starched and stultifying effects. Eventually super-pianists will develop who will play and record with both total command and total abandon.

♭

Nietzsche has designated the opposite poles of the aesthetic cycle as Apollonian and Dionysian. The apostles of Apollo defend the values of craftsmanship, proportion, elegance, and symmetry; disciples of Dionysus dance to the tunes of ecstasy, excess, and a profusion of colorful imagery. The musical code words analogous to these contradictory tendencies are the hoary and expedient terms Classical and Romantic. The casual overuse of these terms has rendered them nearly meaningless. The inconsistencies which abound in their application deny them any integrity, except as the most primitive of modes of description.

For instance, Classical forms and structures are often far more complex and adventurous than the forms of Romantic art, which are typically more symmetrical in their architectural blueprint. What conforms more generally to the stereotypes are but their respective surface textures, Classical lucidity and transparency versus Romantic denseness and embellishment. But even these attributions are dangerous and feed a tired game of dividing both world and idea into opposing camps. Night and day, sun and moon, East and West are inescapable antipodes, but the work of art is ever vigilant to reject convenient and bipolar diagrams of reality. This is why such concepts as Mozart style, Chopin style, or Brahms style are often excuses for artistic complacency, and an opportunity for excising vital considerations which, for the pedantic, may seem too paradoxical or subversive.

§

If one wants to confound the prevailing stylistic platitudes, in particular the disheveled categories of Classical
and Romantic, a little innocent study of an artist like
Vermeer may trigger one's enlightenment. Thus I stare
intently at a copy of the *Artist in His Studio*, which happily
adorns my own studio, but am incapable of understanding
its meaning or structure according to the usual aesthetic
conventions. What I see instead is a barrage of intricate
forms, a surface both palpitating and calm, human expressions both serene and transported, angles and curves, austerity and lushness, pragmatic reality and ephemeral
mystery. What I see is order and disorder, equilibrium and
dissolution, light and dark, sanity and ecstasy, geometry
and free form, reality and transcendence, all in some kind
of mutual tension tenderly wrought.

After such sobering lessons, it seems presumptuous to
chop down artworks into stylistic pigeonholes. Chopin, for
example, is infinitely Classical, infinitely Romantic, and
nullifying both, infinitely wise as a composer. A disciple of
both Apollo and Dionysus, he is a paragon of that creative
disposition which recognizes that method without madness,
statements without questions, assertions without denials,
or forms without twist or warp become slogans and static
vestiges.

Perhaps it is useful to know these ancient categories, but
only as points of departure.

§

Humility is that unprejudiced state of mind which,
emptied of ego, permits us to grasp both the facts and
their spiral of associations. Humility enables us to acknowledge the ambiguous but rooted relationship of fact to
facet, cause to effect, subject to shadow. (Is the shadow a

vestige of the subject, or is it the subject's unblemished outline?)

Humility is premise to that openness and modesty which can see outward and inward without distortion. It is not a mindless genuflection adopted for the chanting of dogmatic rituals, the better to keep things under control. Genuine humility leads to an appreciation of the good life, but it grants the good sense to distinguish close from far, enduring from transient, vital from expedient. Choices are made, but are armed with sufficient insight to recognize that what may appear to be accessory or decorative is quite possibly an essential booster to the basic nucleus—or, more concretely, the nucleus in microcosm.

False humility is often the face of a certain sterility or stubbornness. In musical performance it can express itself in dry, literal readings which curiously may appeal to our "natural" instincts for simplification and self-denial.

♭

A work of art has a genesis, a concrete actuality, and a legacy. To deal with it exclusively as a thing-in-itself, devoid of roots and ramifications, is to confine and eviscerate its potential matrix of associations. Shelley once observed that the poem had already lost some of its inspirational source in the process of being set down on paper. And the intensity of the poem, affecting its interpretation, is surely a coefficient of its meaning for future generations.

The performance of a musical composition cannot ignore the claims of past and future in its consideration of the text. The historical models of prior works and composers, whatever topical allusions, biographical or geographical, psychological or poetic, and the score's prophecies made manifest in later works and commentary must all offer insights and markers for the interpretation. These references need not distract, discolor, or dissemble the mighty icon of the text itself, but rather yield to it dimension and aura, depth and daring.

For the text is not a frozen, immaculate conception. It is a living if dormant tissue activated by the sounding of its notes and their instructions. Every sounding reveals different possibilities and approaches—contingency factors to be neither indulged nor shirked. Why not enjoy the spectrum of variables according to the light of the day, plus past and future days?

ọ

The range and depth of works of art can be measured by their claims on the future. Each new generation discovers meanings in the work of particular significance to its own preoccupations and prejudices. Perhaps no composer more than Bach has spoken in so many different ways to later times and cultures, which in turn have interpreted, arranged, and transcribed his music in every conceivable fashion. The legion of interpretations ventured, free and strict, so-called Classical, Romantic, and "authentic" baroque, is patent testimony to the depth of the music and to its capacity to absorb wounds and blessings from all quarters. The inherent majesty of Bach is in no way compromised, and is even oddly embellished by transcriptions of his music made by certain semi-classical groups and jazz artists. Dating myself, I remember with pleasure the charm of Bach arrangements devised by an elegant pop group known as the Swingle Singers. For any expression of tenderness and craft will be amply repaid by the music's infinite spaciousness.

Interpretation—the unfolding and mediated account of any work—is inexorably conditioned by the temperament of the times. No act of will, no instinct toward preservation or purity can eliminate the inherent bias. (Anatole Broyard advised: Hang on to your prejudices; they are the only taste you've got.) Rather, our energies should be spent in building bridges between the bias and the work, between the work and its latent possibilities.

𝄃

A work of art, if it passes through the portals of "posterity," will generally respond to the needs of the time. Conversely, we may seize upon those particular elements of the work which we believe to be essential prescription or compensation for current ills and distortions. Carl Jung suggested that each generation of artists labors to redress perceived imbalances, both aesthetic and social. In this sense, the purely entertainment values of art are but a handsome cover to its real content, which always includes a polemical, quasi-political component. And even if simple pleasure is the main message, it inclines to promote a greater liberality and decency.

Therefore I do not object to but applaud the efforts of a stage director such as Peter Sellars, who taps the copious sources of Mozart and Handel operas to investigate the predicaments of contemporary life. I may shrink from certain details (perhaps an index of my low threshold of embarrassment), but I feel that Sellars respects the text, and that he explores it to identify the condemnations of social injustice intrinsic to all great art and its just interpretations. When I play a Beethoven sonata, I should like to bring out a similar appeal for the attitudes of tolerance which inhabit its pages.

𝄃

Sometimes the legacy of a work is not all that benign or reassuring. When I work on the *Dante* Sonata by Liszt (as well as other of his compositions), I detect strange omens of the modern temper: anxiety, anarchy, nihilism, even varieties of annihilation. Notwithstanding its moments of redemption, there is a grinding madness in this piece not specific to Dante's inferno, but smelling of gulags, the machines of war, as well as that vertigo and emptiness reminiscent of contemporary visions of hell.

Did Liszt intend this? Therefore, how valid is my inference? Wrong, in that he could not have imagined the exponential misery and destructiveness of modern war (although the decimating rattle of machine guns may yet be heard); right, in that his specter of doom was sufficiently grotesque and nameless to invite images of all the loathsome progeny of contemporary evil. Regardless, when performing this work one articulates, voluntarily or involuntarily, those images most urgent to this time, with no intention of contradicting the score but rather demonstrating its breadth and implications.

Such works cover a wide territory. It is easy to get lost. One is constantly groping, but grateful for the range of meanings.

♮

Stop, look, and listen! Is it possible that a belief in inclusiveness can go too far? That by opening all doors it may provoke a wretched excess which discards basic propriety and gazes on its own navel in existential bliss? Or welcomes those scruffy hoodlums and puffy dowagers who bloat the sound, derange the style, and substitute thud and blunder for blood and thunder? After all, Goethe said that there is nothing more dreadful than imagination without taste.

I have heard such arbitrary and indulgent pianists, albeit they are but a tiny fraction of their stolid and conventional club. It may not always be fun to hear them, but the ultimate standard of acceptability is persistent and absolute. Do they respect the score, its markings and map? Or do they ride roughshod over it, spear waving, sense departed in pursuit of the brass ring and dreams of victory?

One might add that Einstein (Albert) said that imagination is more important than knowledge. Then let us split the difference and suggest that taste and knowledge should refine imagination, and that imagination should invigorate taste and knowledge. The simple truth (not so simple to gauge) is that untrammeled imagination can lead to indiscriminate inclusiveness, while informed taste will emphasize the conclusive and compelling images. The exchange is dynamic in both directions, but it is nice to start with more than with less. Better the variety of life than a fixed and miserly share.

Or: taste without imagination dwindles to tastefulness.

𝄢

Given the carnival of the day, its pop culture and brazen chronicle, it may be surprising to note (or unsurprising, if Jung's theory of compensation is correct) that the temper of many current artistic expressions is relatively conservative, cryptic, or genteel. Some of these trends include minimalism in painting and music, constructivism in sculpture, and a general neo-Romanticism throughout art, although sometimes in rather insipid versions. Only serious fiction, refusing the easy concessions to accessibility, still seems to be pursued by the ghosts of Joyce and Faulkner.

Of course generalizations will not do, and the many exceptions must spoil the rule. Nevertheless, in musical performance the interpretive approach for many decades, perhaps beginning to change now, has been somber and faithful, generic and unexceptional. Unity is substantially favored over variety (one tempo per movement is the miserly allowance), and the protagonists of "Less is more" have won the recent battles.

I have never quite understood how less can be more. It seems to me that more is more, and that having all the colors of the spectrum to choose from is more advantageous than having a few or two of them, no matter that one or two are superficially more coherent than many. Does it have something to do with reductive scientific or religious paradigms? Or with the character of modern audiences, always in a hurry to ingest and depart? Or is it the residue from powerful musicians a half century ago who would purge music of excess and rhetoric? Or is it the effect of recordings, clinging to the center of gravity? Or is it simply the universal need to calm down after a century of madness?

♩

There is much evidence to suggest that composers of the Classical period intended for their slow movements to move in leisurely, flowing tempi, and in general *less* slowly than contemporary practice would dictate. For recent generations (and, alas, myself), the slow movements have often become the occasion for varieties of revelation, their undiluted piety a fragile thread to heaven and therefore vulnerable to sudden shock or undue momentum.

For my own Viennese mentors, too slow was an invitation to disaster, rather the sign of cloistered minds taking refuge in quasi-mystical clichés, and, more important, resulting in a kind of metric (and expressive) quicksand which deprived the tempo of sufficient flow to sustain the structure. By their reckoning, and as well the testimony of pertinent metronome markings left by Beethoven (and his student Czerny), Classical composers did not at all share the predilection of Wagner, who advised that the tempo of a slow movement could never be slow enough. One is reminded here of the old adage which contrasts the respective temperaments of the Viennese and the Germans: the Germans say the situation is serious but not hopeless; the Viennese say the situation is hopeless but not serious.

When Rachmaninoff was asked by a conductor to choose the tempo for the slow movement in one of his concerti, he is supposed to have replied, Not too slow; I am not a Beethoven specialist.

ȸ

One day when in my teens, I played the Beethoven Piano Sonata, op. 109, for my lesson. The last movement is a set of variations based upon a theme of gentle, stately flow. The character of the movement is quite extraordinary, an ecstatic, fruitful, smiling homage to the benevolent Creator, never austere and as relevant to the good earth as to the kind angel. It is marked Andante: flowing and singing, not at all static, but with an embracing warmth.

I was playing it rather too deliberately, however, and my teacher quite understandably objected. With more courage than I anticipated, I struggled to defend my choice of tempo, trying to point out that in our shell-shocked universe, these kinds of blessed statements required a slower pace to seduce the attention of mind and audience. It was as though such tender and personal thoughts required a cordon of impenetrable serenity around them to survive intact. And the psychic claims of our lives here and now justified the more deliberate tempo.

To my surprise, my dear and demanding teacher shrugged his shoulders and said, "All right, do it your way." He could be merciless (though never harsh) if one was motivated by indulgence or vapid indifference. In this case he deferred, however, and since then I play this movement slower or faster, torn between the poles of "authenticity" and cultural exigency—or one's presumptions thereof.

ᦔ

Time is the path by which we measure our failures and successes. It is inexorable, neutral, and user-unfriendly. It has but one dimension, a monorail to oblivion on a straight track assembled of equal segments. In music, it is the province of meter, constant and inherently unaffected by the pleas of songbirds and diffuse landscapes.

Or, time is the motif of diction and its scansions. By the pattern of its articulations and groupings, character is imprinted, characters of grace and doom, of perky dances and brooding soliloquies. It is the province of rhythm, and it announces itself in combinations of short and long durations which sit astride the meter, sometimes comfortably, sometimes rakishly, or swooning at an angle.

Or, time is memory, dreams, and prophecy. It moves backward and forward, away from reality, into visions of release and transcendence. Line and melody author this dreamworld where reckoning is indifferent to the clicks of linear time but committed to the caprices and debts of the psyche. Timelessness is the condition to which it aspires.

Or, time is the setting sun, the tides, the cycles of light and dark, the shifting moods of our lives. These displacing textures belong essentially to the domain and timely progression of the harmonies. This time and all the other facets of time must mesh and coexist in the unfolding of music.

ᦔ

In music, time is a network of several coordinates with diverse inclinations. It is not exclusively beat-beat-beat, which is but one of the variables. The variables interact, compromising none of them in theory, although musical syntax requires concessions and adjustments to maintain equilibrium. The interests of all combined must be served. For instance, nothing is more touching than the chemistry of plaintive time in absentminded thrall supported by a sympathetic but unyielding accompaniment. The coordination of metric insistence, however gentle, with melismatic ardor becomes a paradigm for life's inextinguishable hopes and resignations.

But in an even more fundamental sense time is the central preoccupation of music. For time unmediated is the stuff and drone of reality, so dim-witted that it can only proceed one pace at a time. Music is born to subvert this monotonous absence of eloquence. For music conceives many times and timings, if only, at a minimum, through its changing tempi; each tempo institutes a different reordering of pace, until time becomes the friendly bearer of every mood and activity comprehensible to humans, from the flights of near entropy to the flights of atoms and bumblebees. Time is thus seduced by the protean gifts of human imagination. Through music time is tamed, although music never forgets to remind us of time's faceless mission.

§

It is like a play. Various characters of various persuasions mingle and debate their special interests, basically a trio, but each of the three has different voices and personae. All the characters participate in the general thesis and well-being; there are no strident disagreements. It is more like examining an idea from different perspectives, some more lucid, others more obscure but no less functional to the whole.

The characters symbolize certain roles within the universe they share and represent: aspects of the individual, the collective, the motion, the setting. There are no heroes and no villains, but heroic and tragic tales are told. Comedy and farce, all the kin of Romeo and Juliet, northern lights, southern fountains, the idea as will, as play, as diagram of hell and heaven, these all belong to the repertoire of this traveling theater.

The main characters are (1) line, sometimes known as melody or motive, and its siblings of counterpoint; (2) harmony, which has two masks, one active, idiomatic, and generating, the other the passive collection of the whole; (3) time, which subdivides into many species, from relentless to random. Together these three actors grind and merge into portraits of all that is knowable and expressible.

$$\wr$$

Of course music cannot formulate the principles behind the description of quarks, the fourth dimension, or superstrings (unless one refers to old recordings of the Philadelphia Orchestra). Quarks? Well, Beethoven has provided rather sophisticated examples of the immutable but convertible nature of building blocks and ground motives. The fourth dimension?

Child's play for music. Space—a function of the transparency to density curve, expressed acoustically, rhetorically, and by the sheer chemistry of sounds in combination—grapples with Hydra-headed time, from which conflict perturbations arise that dislocate the coordinates native to each. As line steers through this Scylla and Charybdis, adding a third factor of reference and will, subtle or broad contingencies develop spontaneously which introduce fourth and fortuitous dimensions to the otherwise static trio. The terms of the conversation, heated or tender, are constantly subject to transient discoveries that affect the course of the whole.

This is performance as it should be, improvising, dynamic, and startling, but at ease with the conditionality of being. Only within such a volatile mix can the lyrical voice, quiet and consoling, be truly apprehended.

ọ

One method of distinguishing the compositional approaches of Liszt and Chopin, and by extension their respective visions of technique, would be to compare the design of their passagework, in particular the cadenzas of grace notes both interpolate so frequently. It is perhaps fair to say that the cadenzas in Liszt are more celebrations of harmonic and rhetorical functions; in Chopin they are rather elaborations of melodic ideas. Therefore the patterns in Chopin's cadenzas are often more intricate insofar as they replicate and develop nuances of the motive; while for Liszt the prescriptions of harmonic content determine the lift and limits of the passage. Since Liszt inserts the cadenza for primarily rhetorical reasons, the melodic mosaic used to fill out the time zone may seem rather predictable, belonging to one of a relative handful of public-domain figurations to which Liszt is disposed.

These considerations suggest the possibility that the technical discourse in Liszt issues from a file of prescribed patterns of enormous but essentially additive difficulty. In Chopin the patterns are more articles of lyrical and motivic invention, spun into supple and crystalline arabesques.

These surmises on technique and style would do potential disservice to Liszt if implying tactical limitations to his handling of motivic materials. Another dubious impression would suggest that Chopin is inherently a miniaturist by contrast to Liszt, who concerns himself with grander themes. Needless to say, any such conjectures would be presumptuous in the face of creative genius.

Less speculative, however, is the comparison of the separate models of the hand. For Chopin the hand is a collection of fluid inequities to be exploited for the variations of touch necessary to articulate the many aspects of melodic contour, as well as the harmonic and contrapuntal textures supporting or contrasting the line. For Liszt the hand is a highly mobilized if less idiomatic force for carving out and distributing the dramatic tableau.

The emerging and the finished professional alike need reference to both models of the hand to play the piano.

♩

Several years ago the A-flat Polonaise of Chopin climbed to the top of the hit parade for a considerable spell. The most famous recording of that time (along with its many imitations) seemed to exemplify the inherent grandeur and dignity of the work. Throughout, one was keenly conscious of the noble rhetoric, of the stately pacing which embodied the very spirit of the dance and its manifestly patriotic nature.

By chance I happened to hear an old recording of the piece from three generations ago. The pianist was a remarkably versatile artist, Leopold Godowsky, a composer, a prolific transcriber, and an inventor on the side. I was quite astonished by the approach and spirit of this performance. Suddenly there was a lithe agility, a quick and resilient tempo, an idiomatic and frisky handling of the tune, above all a sparkling élan which knocked all the stuffing and chauvinism out of the piece, making it breathe with the joy of battle, the charm of gender, and the lessons of humor, a blessed, reborn, bumptious, bouncy humor full of satire, tease, and twinkle.

There is the French Chopin, more classical; there is the Polish Chopin, more passionate. That is the easy diagram.

More significantly, there is the Chopin who is inventive, who is wily, who is magisterial, and who has more disguises, foils, and sabers than all the nobility he adored and detested.

♀

We have gotten used to a Chopin style which is not so much sentimental at heart but sentimental in spirit, where a kindly and spacious languor prevails as a stereotype of Romantic yearning. Clearly this style is currently favored, notwithstanding those incisive passages and pieces which demand (and receive) a brisk, energetic execution. One remembers that Chopin was a less than successful performer, allegedly because his tone was too weak to be heard beyond the first few rows. Was it a matter of weakness then, or rather of a subtlety and intricacy too fine to be digested? How much is this problem compounded by the modern phenomenon of even larger halls? Or by the modern temper, used to grand, reductive solutions, primary colors, patent cues and labels?

One bar, one of almost any in Chopin, will reveal the extraordinary refinements teeming with life, with the multiple inflections of sound and meaning that are the norm in his music. For instance, the first bar from the middle episode of the F-sharp Major Nocturne, op. 15, no. 2, vividly attests to the variety of textures required. Within a typically homophonic framework, the right-hand melody is contrived of no less than three separate voices, while the left-hand accompaniment must also deal with three different touches, one for each sonority struck. The effect should be well modulated, but must reflect the entire constellation of interests and nuances indicated. And this within a mood of tender buoyancy.

There is much devil in this deep blue sea. Most of it is

beneath the surface, but transparent purpose and touch make it audible.

𝆑

We have always had this rather civilized civil war between Mozart and Haydn defenders. Nobody takes this very seriously, for why choose between scotch and bourbon when both are failproof and make the dream team to paradise? Perhaps that's the rub. Mozart, they say, travels in the higher spheres, protected from cranks, bores, riddles, warts, upsets, sores, and gridlock by those serene preserves of infallible taste and celestial wisdom which grace him. Mozart is Little Lord Fauntleroy grown up, immune from the stings of adolescence and the slings of middle age. Without Mozart the ad agency for angels would lose its leading model, and the festivals which wallow in his name would lose their altar boy, who bestows peace and chocolates to audiences hassled by life.

For many who are dedicated consumers of music, Mozart confirms the sacraments of goodwill and gracious living. He embodies the conviction which advocates everything in moderation except the enjoyment of life. Mozart knows that the divine itself is but that state of enlightenment which blesses man's natural and pleasurable instincts, though divinely graced.

Is this an accurate picture of the real Mozart?

𝆑

As for Haydn, he is considered a far more earthy fellow (although the extravagant claims and stereotypes of *Amadeus*, movie and play, tend to negate the contrast between the two). Haydn, after all, was the chap who expressed much pride and pleasure when the shot he fired killed one partridge and then pierced another, two for the price of one. If Mozart delighted in the wine of life (as well as women and song), Haydn was more of a Joe Six-pack, armed with sturdy piety and a laconic wit for adjusting to the gruff realities. For Haydn, native piety was not merely a convention. He would pray on his knees, usually with success, for divine inspiration, but if the ideas did not come, then a second heavenly appeal would invariably work.

Needless to say, both of these portraits are naive and overdrawn. Haydn has written some of the most ethereal music imaginable, as mystical and unearthly as certain paintings by Watteau. At the same time, Mozart can be quite bitter and brittle; some passages have a raucous humor and lacerating intensity akin to Bartók's.

There are several layers of activity in all good music, psychological and compositional. Which layers are exposed and which are concealed vary in displacement according to individual creative will. The rhetoric of Haydn goes across the board and, relatively speaking, unites all layers in common purpose for uncommon deed. More precisely, rhetoric and structure coincide. Mozart is far more surreptitious. The friendly exterior veils active strains of disturbance and detour, doubt and defiance.

𝄞

The Piano Sonata in C Minor, composed in 1771 and identified in the catalogue as Hoboken 20, furnishes potent evidence of Haydn's rhetorical and structural freedom. As an example of his so-called Sturm und Drang period, wherein expressive values are prominently and uncompromisingly featured, it is generally assumed that this work is less representative of a more mature style, which tends to pacify the storms and level the outbursts. But in fact the inherent predisposition of Haydn to ruffle the forms and break up the normal continuities of sense and structure is fully evident in many works throughout his entire output.

In the C Minor Sonata the atmosphere of turbulence, even terror, is more feverishly pitched, but the path of establishing order through a series of dislocations and their responses is not at all anomalous to his general rules of procedure.

The first four bars of the first movement do not stray from the ordinary rules of engagement, although they betray a dark and passionate question incapable of glib response. The fifth bar starts like the first, but an octave lower. At that point the logical expectation is denied, even shattered. The sixth bar dislocates the register, contracts the argument, and yields a passage that intensifies both syncopation and thought by chopping the discourse into angry or hungry gasps, then leading to a cadence forlorn with regret and resignation.

The expressive gloss offered here may be fanciful, but the musical facts are self-evident. It would be futile to deny them a dramatic source or scenario.

♀

The broken promises and structural disjunctions of this opening phrase in the Haydn C Minor Piano Sonata nevertheless manage to fit within the ordinary eight-bar standard. As all great artists are inclined, especially the composers of the Classical era, the disturbing and subversive implications of their art become more compelling, as both time bomb and portrait of reality, when the untidy material is neatly wrapped in conventional packages. That is how they achieve the impossible, squaring the circle.

From another perspective, the inherent conflict and dynamic between the ribs of conventional form and the materials of untrammeled, eruptive life are cogently illuminated by the commentaries on rhythm found in the notebooks of Gerard Manley Hopkins. He contrasts routine "running rhythm," with its regular feet and accents, to "sprung rhythm," which he defines as "the native and natural rhythm of speech, the least forced, the most rhetorical and emphatic of all possible rhythms, combining opposite . . . and incompatible excellences." Superimposing sprung rhythm onto running, regulated rhythm yields that counterpoint of process expressed by sudden accident or revelation puncturing routine existence, by the contrasting grammars of prose and poetry, by the contradictions native to art itself, or, in spectacular fashion, by the deconstructions of Haydn. In his music the collision between precedent and accident is of unparalleled audacity.

♩

After the first eight-bar period in the C Minor Sonata, a transition comprising two three-bar phrases, identical but for harmonic orientation, leads to the second theme. In fulfilling its innocuous, predictable task, this transition is anything but. Without attempting a play-by-play account, suffice it to say that the musical material is both lean and dense, ornate and simple, stressed and meandering, loud and soft, articulate and diffuse, purposeful and vague, formed and formless. What Haydn lets in the side door— a kind of "uncertainty principle"—exits gracefully through the front door. Uncertainty, or accident, is not a disease, but a condition of development and evolution.

One might object to the anachronistic transplant of the uncertainty principle onto the robust contours of Haydn's musical will. For what he composes seems to have its own compass and direction as it confidently heads for shore. Perhaps more determined than confident, for in fact the route is circuitous, and as many theologians have commented, all grappling with faith or idea is racked with contingency and doubt.

Creative artists have always been able to anticipate the future mindscape and landscape. For instance, one thinks of Thomas Hardy's portrait of the cultural universe a century ago, in which uncertainty, chaos, the random, the unsettling were all powerful players. One is amazed and thankful that Haydn managed to integrate these presumably dark, manic forces into visions of prayer and optimism.

♀

Speaking of prayer, it is difficult to think of a reverie of such tender betrothal to the genies of kindness, flow, and abandon as offered by the second movement of this sonata. Lines as long and gently curved as the horizon set sail in minute, stepwise scales interpolated and embellished by trills that dissolve all partitions and boundaries. Of course everything must be executed with a thousand and one filaments of nuance; no careening *rubato* can steer this vessel. Only a gentle absorption of the sun's rays and a gentle shaping of the phrase will propel ship and text, marked *andante con moto*, neither slow nor fast, neither real nor unreal.

But every music is bound by music's language, which in turn is bound by its guidelines and catechisms. Even this reverie subdivides into grace notes, dotted rhythms, rests, sixteenths, slurs, and all the rest; and this unpatriarchal family of articulations presided over by Papa Haydn must observe filial respect to the canon of notational meanings and distinctions. All music, but in particular music of the Classical style, is retrievable only by its loyalty to the articulations. The Classical ethos, imbued with the codes and chatter of argument, dialectics, and exchanges of information, depends upon precise formulations of touches and groupings in all sizes. Thus the timeless barcarolle of this

not-so-slow movement speaks yet in wavelets, curls, and
eddies as defined and delicate as they are spacious.

𝄾

The third movement of this sonata is pure deviltry, equal
parts funny and grotesque. A detail I admire as sample of
the whole, and sample of the psyche of this mad and capricious philosopher, is found in the second statement of
the principal theme (beginning with the upbeat to bar 7),
where the chords which filled out the downbeats of the first
two bars in the original statement of this theme have been
assassinated this second time around. Just like that, bang,
they are gone, and in their place there is nothing but a
big, fat, gaping hole. Why this toothless gap? Why this
disdainful void? To further derange bruised spirits? To further collapse our hold on reality? To leave us more vulnerable to the pitch and yaw of fate's conditionality, to
centerless whimsy?

Well, perhaps it's only a temporary derangement in pursuit of a compositional tactic. For the hole thins the general
texture, liberates the solo "fiddle," and allows the phrase
to fly out the window, relatively traceless. The archprank-
ster, Haydn, shoots his arrow, removes the evidence, and
disappears. And out of every vacuum new threads and
branchings arise. The trajectory of thought is stirred by
ideas and by their absence as well.

Courage. The wit and courage to leave this hole, confront
the emptiness, and trust that God abhors a vacuum and
will fill it with beans and holly. Less melodramatically
speaking, the gardeners call it pruning.

𝄾

The didacts of purity who like their Mozart interpretations sweet and simple gain supporting evidence from his
letters, which often invoke standards of tastefulness, discre-

tion, and balance. For instance, in 1777 he writes to his father, "Everyone praised my beautiful, pure tone." And then again to his father in 1781, ". . . as passions, whether violent or not, must never be expressed in such a way as to invite disgust, and as music, even in the most terrible situations, must never cease to be MUSIC . . ." Then there is the famous comment about his rival Clementi, whom he dismisses as a "mere *mechanicus*," possessing not "a farthing's worth of taste."

In the area of physical gesture and decorum, Mozart is no less explicit in his parody of the antics of an eight-year-old prodigy: "For instead of sitting in the middle of the clavier, she sits right opposite the treble, as it gives her more chance of flopping about and making grimaces. She rolls her eyes and smirks. When a passage is repeated, she plays it even more slowly. When a passage is being played, the arm must be raised as high as possible, and according as the notes in the passage are stressed, the arm, not the fingers, must do this, and that too with great emphasis in a heavy and clumsy manner."

From these and corresponding remarks, can anyone question the primacy of taste and refinement, clarity and elegance in Mozart's pantheon of musical values? Or his father's values?

♩

Of course there are other sides to Mozart's personality, artistic and human. We know that he liked to gamble, that he wrote scatological and "nonsense" letters to a favorite cousin, and that he participated in the mystical rituals of the Masonic brotherhood. Most revealing, perhaps, are the nonsense letters, which express unalloyed pleasure in deconstructing the conventional meaning and sequence of words and grammar by devices of wild punning, exaggeration, and farce. There is much partiality toward riddles and shaggy-dog stories, and toward a word assembly that mocks familiar usage by devices of aimless repetition or dissociation, of the sort that hints at tactics cultivated by modern writers such as Beckett or Robbe-Grillet. By reiterating ordinary locutions with but the slightest variations of stress and diction, Mozart exposes the content of social exchanges and relationships as fragile, habitual, spurious, and, lurking in the background, unjust. By his subtle manipulations of verbal inflection, the platitudinous thoughts of the day become absurd or rebellious; meaning is habit, and when habit is stretched thin by ramble or ridicule, then meaning has no more substance than the emperor's clothes.

Does this imply that Mozart was a closet revolutionary or a Swiftian cynic? No more than to the degree that all artists are revolutionaries. Some exploit crucifixes, while others, like Mozart, confound reality by exposing it—to make nonsense of its sense. Or is it the other way around?

♩

Mozart was naturally and genetically disposed toward accepting the musical conventions of his time. And what his genes did not determine, the musical training by his father assured. Given the intensity of that education, so thorough and competent, the devoted compliance of the young child was not unexpected. Before puberty Mozart had already assimilated the laws and language of musical construction, from which he produced stunning examples in both performance and composition. Because he was already in control of the means of production, the shape of future creations depended only upon variables of fate and personality, both notoriously quirky, however, according to individual circumstances.

The philosophical content of Mozart's response to these variables is expressed most conspicuously in his operas.

Though wrapped in the mantle of stylistic conventions, their subject matter addresses the vivid and provocative imponderables of gender, caste, and creation. Of their daring, the reaction of Berlioz—who declared that he would give his right arm if Mozart had not composed *Don Giovanni*, given a subject so unworthy and licentious—presents unambiguous testimony. Are we, as indiscriminate secularists, insensitive to such insinuations and subversions? With few exceptions, at either end of the political spectrum, we are unlikely to notice such "dangerous" implications, a fact that makes one wonder if our performances of Mozart in general have not lost some spark of rebellion or just plain mischief. For too easily consecrated, Mozart becomes a symbol of complacency as well as of the divine.

♭

If we are looking for the spirit of play, for the play of ideas and perspectives, and for a freedom which may explore hidden paths without willfully violating established canons, then we must find it in the syntax and forms of Mozart's music. No gestures of braggadocio, no purple patches, no brazen or ominous harmonies can act as surrogates of this freedom; only the actual deployment of notes, phrases, and forms can function as determinants of vital activity and invention.

Once, when young and green, I complained to my teacher about the structure of a Mozart sonata then under study. While playing it through at the lesson, I made some bratty remarks about its predictable form, just eight-bar phrases one after another all lined up in harmless sequence. For reasons I badly misunderstood as tacit approval, Mr. Steuermann smiled indulgently and let me go on. Now I realize that he simply did not wish to discuss a subject too subtle and beyond my years.

For example, on the local level, the correct reading of

the second theme, first movement, from the G Minor Piano Quartet has been the source of intense controversy engaged in by many leading musicians, including Schoenberg. A phrase of four bars in four-quarter time has been fitted by Mozart with a pattern of slurs and accents sufficiently ambiguous to invite several plausible interpretations. It is far too complicated to describe satisfactorily, but the residue of this controversy contributes to an interesting and operative maxim pertinent to almost all Mozart themes, in that they possess a degree of flexibility which allows for different scansions, different readings, and different emotional inflections.

The corollary and more general maxim states that nothing is as simple as it seems, especially in Mozart.

ρ̨

The curious elusiveness of this particular theme from the G Minor Piano Quartet, what makes it so hard to scan and decipher, is exceptional only to the *degree* of its topographical whimsy. If this theme were wildly anomalous to the general menu of Mozart melodies, then one could hold its wayward mix of articulation signs (and the asymmetrical groupings they signify) responsible. But if this theme were representative, admittedly in striking and concentrated fashion, of the tendency of all Mozart themes, then some process of alchemy, however disguised, would be constantly and functionally at work.

The theme we are discussing (tentatively, as its complexity permits) can be divided roughly into two segments: three bars of question (antecedent) and one bar of answer (consequent). The tag-end bar concluding the phrase is unexceptional but for its relation to the whole. Together these four bars fulfill the general Mozartean ethic and standard of inspired, freethinking, non-Euclidean, multidimensional themes, achieved by a variety of means of which one is particularly characteristic and remarkable. The pattern of accents and rhythmic durations confers special emphasis upon four specific notes within the four bars; in the context of the four-quarter meter, each of these stresses falls on a different beat of each bar. Keeping in mind that the theme actually begins on the third beat, in succession the third, the fourth, the second, and the first beats of their respective bars carry the accented load. Of course, some accents are more significant than others, but it is this general strategy of freely distributing the rhythmic (and motivic) weight throughout all the metric elements of the phrase which gives the music its distinctive lilt and gallantry.

By extension, among the two or more (in the F Major Piano Sonata, K. 332, seven!) themes in Mozart expositions, the rhythmic emphasis will generally tend to focus on a different beat for each respective theme. Thus every beat of the given meter is activated throughout by this complementary distribution. The meter itself, then, is constantly rejuvenated by this sharing of the spoils.

ḥ

To appreciate the Mozartean formula and gift in perspective, it should be observed that there are specific, discernible differences in compositional ethic and procedure between Mozart and Haydn. Haydn exploits an economy of means, developing continuations and ideas from the configurations and resources of the principal theme. The consequences are clear: the second theme of his expositions is often a direct descendant of the first theme with but minor alterations. As well, in Haydn the development section of the sonata form is generally a more active and radioactive territory, deliberately the locus and center for compressing, carving, and recasting materials from the exposition.

In Mozart the development section is typically less adventurous in its disposition of the original and germinal ideas. On some occasions even, a "new" theme may appear in the development, on the face of it a theoretical violation of the prescriptions for sonata-allegro form. Of course, this new theme is usually not new at all but rather a skeleton or apparition of a previous idea transformed, diffused, defused to fit Mozart's conception of the larger form.

For Haydn the development area is more a center of intrigue, a commerce of ideas experimentally traded, truncated, or re-fused into new shapes. For Mozart, so fertile and abundant in his expositions, the development is more like a holding zone, more a respite than a marketplace. Mostly reprints or impressions of the initial material remain, and in between the vivid expositions and their recapitulations a certain truce is maintained. Needless to say, there are exceptions.

♭

Before abandoning the discussion on the role of the development section, it would be useful to address a related topic currently (and eternally) debated. What are the criteria for observing or dispensing with the repeat signs affixed to expositions in sonata movements of the (mostly) Classical period? Leading musicians have recently presented their arguments for and against playing the repeat in the forum of influential literary journals. It makes for a stimulating inquiry, involving several contingency factors that apply. Among these are (1) our cumulative familiarity with the materials of such expositions as derived from exposure to these sonatas over the years, arguing against the repeat; (2) the duration of the repeated material as it affects pragmatic considerations of length of piece and program, arguing either way; (3) whether actual written-out music was left by the composer distinguishing the first from the second ending (the practice of Schubert), arguing generally in behalf of the repeat. Nevertheless, one crucial factor that has not been sufficiently addressed concerns the effect of the repeat, or non-repeat, on the dramatic function of the development section, as a matter of both psychology and form.

Developments, whether reflecting either of the diverse conceptions of Mozart or Haydn, offer perspectives entirely different from those of the surrounding principalities of exposition and recapitulation. Instead, they are arenas of adventure, of inquest and reformulation. Their mission is not to "expose" the material (other than in the deconstructing sense) but to question, disarm, and explode it into new arrangements and codes which derail the original shape and sequence of ideas. The dramatic impact of this transformation is heightened by repeating the exposition, generally speaking. Not in all circumstances, perhaps, as according to the contingency factors, but by stabilizing and "seconding" the original material, the sheer novelty of the development as a laboratory of change is further illumined. By this double grounding of first principles, the very concept of development—as will, evolution, flight—is more starkly displayed and liberated.

♀

If the development sections of Mozart are more a period of grace and disarmament than a time of upheaval, it is of course not the result of any deficiencies in his techniques of elaboration. Mozart developed his material in a different way, through the internal semantics of individual themes and—what is exceptionally interesting, subtle, and related—through the interplay and compensating features deployed among the entire set of themes in any given movement.

For Mozart, no moment in the architecture of the move-

ment was so insignificant as not to warrant a motive or
theme attached of appropriate charm and profile. The most
meager, functional transitions (often these especially) were
blessed with tunes of distinction which only contributed to
the general abundance.

But quite apart from the exquisite balancings and dis-
tributions within the individual themes, another elegant
process of differentiation and organization was occurring on
a more cumulative level. A larger dialogue among the
several themes ensued, as their individual characteristics
both matched and compensated for each other. Strands of
thought and of the given motivic cells would be shared,
while new shapes would develop which filled in unexplored
(but implied, if by omission) elements of previous (or pro-
spective) themes. A general concert of ideas would be distributed among the member themes, each fulfilling a stage
of the glorious equation crowning the whole.

This was indeed development, in the sense of related and
evolving creatures of the same species—that species inhab-
iting and organic to the given piece.

ρ

The developmental process in Haydn is rhetorical in the
sense of clarifying and underlining the argument, and dialectical in the sense of announcing, rejecting, and recasting
the ideas. In Mozart the process is more subtle and more
difficult to describe. The same tools of imitation, compres-
sion, extension, and conversion are evident but not as intentionally manifest. Instead, there is a kaleidoscopic vision
which views the entire product from on high, and by virtue
of its casual magnanimity and patrician deftness multiplies
and distributes the ground ideas throughout the entire
movement and population. Every poor and rich moment of
the form participates in the melodic feast, and each tune is

half sibling to the others. There is a dazzling yet subterranean exchange of materials, with certain intervals and stresses redeploying periodically while their counterparts, inversions, and alter egos emerge in turn to rectify the balance.

What we have on the surface is a monarchy, in that the general demeanor of style and expression obeys the traditional dictates. Under the surface we have a thriving, honeycombed democracy, where each is nourished according to his or her needs, and everybody eats cake.

ò

In the first movement of the aforementioned F Major Piano Sonata, we have a patent yet "guileless" example of this affluence of contrasting and collaborating themes so pervasive in Mozart. In the exposition of this movement there are seven different and alluring themes, of which the so-called principal theme, subordinate theme, and closing theme areas share six of them, yet leaving the most elaborate to the transition connecting the regions of principal and second themes. In addition, the opening and closing themes each subdivide internally into two distinct portions of discrete, identifiable motives.

The connections, overlaps, and responses among the welter of sources in this movement would require pages of prose and diagrams to articulate. The fundamental byplay is along two channels. On the motivic level there is a continuous colloquy between a pattern of spaced intervals that have an undulating, singsong contour which is then contrasted with sets of the same repeated pitch, usually in groups of three. These complementary motivic lines of endeavor form a thread or matrix of information by which some essential, "genetic" code supersedes the surface plot of lovely tunes laid side by side.

At the same time there is a parallel rhythmic scheme which yields another core of connective and developmental fiber. For the first three bars of the opening theme are absent of notes sounding on the second beat of the ¾ meter. From then on, this given bias in favor of the first and third beats demands constant compensation for the missing second beat, so that all ensuing material is engaged in the rooted conversation caused by this initial void. As typical in Mozart, the ongoing dialogue becomes a festive occasion for discovering those particular melodies and configurations appropriate to this charmed debate.

♭

The development section of this movement affords a splendid glimpse of Mozart's wise and deferential nature, and, as well, his methods of elaboration. Its first eight bars, then repeated an octave lower with but minor variations, display an elegant abstraction and metamorphosis, which incorporate elements from several themes of the exposition into the forging of an apparently new melody. Of course "new" is but a relative term, for nothing is really new which is the consequence of prior causes. And so this is a new-old melody, a fresh face with old bones, or an old face with a new hat. Most remarkable, perhaps the ultimate stroke of genius, is the absolutely placid emotional atmosphere which accompanies this extravagant calculus of ideas, wherein the plumage of so many themes is woven so quietly, so inconspicuously together. There is no stress, no strain, no trauma. The seeds of complementarity have been so gracefully prepared and distributed that the fusion, while tender and prayerful, seems but the most casual, natural event. The internal rhythmic and motivic dialogues are still expressive and redolent, but have been subsumed into a family get-together to which distant cousins and aunts and uncles have been cordially invited. Grace is said, the menu is vegetarian, and all is healthy and varied.

ọ

There is one other aspect of Mozart's compositional and piano style which tends to be overlooked and underexecuted. Passing by in the breeze are his ever so humble accompaniments, supporting the melodies as effortlessly as the most unobtrusive male dancer supports the prima ballerina. In actual performance these accompaniments, which are largely inherited from the general fund—i.e., using figures and figurations readily available to all composers— often sound neither shaped nor sensitive, but rather register only on the channel responsible for keeping time. The harmonic and contrapuntal implications are buried under the clippety-clap.

Yet reason as well as experience dictate that these figures, however impersonal on the surface, are no less part of the discourse, and of an inspiration worthy of that discourse. For you cannot have an inspired melody and a humdrum accompaniment unless you work incompetently on Tin Pan Alley.

In fact the implementation of these figures, wherever they occur in his music, epitomizes Mozart's skill and mastery. They provide overt and covert commentary to the main voice by deft constructions that support, imitate, or complement the line, and yet they are sufficiently independent to offer contrapuntal relief. On the transparency curve they both carry the harmonic content while yet permitting the treble melodies to emerge unscathed. These accompaniments have many duties, from bringing up baby to doing the housework. But they are personalized and buoyant, and will respond only to the most subtle touch and awareness.

♭

These speculations on the psychology and charm of
Mozart's music have inevitable consequences for its interpretation, and for the techniques, approaches, and sonorities
necessary to bring it to full flower and meaning.

Where are we now in our current standards of Mozart
performance? We tend to present Mozart as token and evidence of some divine balm, such that we often hear performances that seem divinely embalmed. A long, sweeping,
but rather static *cantilena* dominates the proceedings, covering the particles of information, curio, and dialogue with
a noble and creamy curve. (Nor does the employment of a
spurious, unvarying *non legato* touch—as style token—
cover the syntactical deficiencies.) Angels are imported from
Raphael to support this parabola, which convinces us of the
sweetness of Mozart's heart while endorsing the friendly,
genteel instincts of mankind. In the fast and brilliant movements we usually hear a lively *spritz*, which is more the
outcome of technical *brio* than conversational aplomb.

The wit, finesse, and repartee of these scores cannot be
realized without attention and love for their articulations.
Accents, slurs, rhythms, lines, balances must be calibrated
according to the indications and implications of the text.
Ultimately one must hear the humor, the bittersweet, the
elegant and quixotic exchanges, the patter, the nonsense,
the tender surprises, the free gift of universal health care,
of cakes and ale, of affection for all. And for this one needs
pogo sticks as well as gliders.

♭

The message and ideal of Mozart is not that easy to
discover in a superficial age which relies upon clichés of
nationalism and piety for its moral backbone. The ax-
iomatic imperative advanced by our respective gods is to

love—thyself, thy family, thy neighbor, thy country, thy stranger and enemy. This is a task we have seriously botched. Normal, therefore partial and partisan, people find it very difficult, indeed impossible, to dispense freely and universally this precious panacea of love.

Mozart lowers the stakes in a very sensible way. While he is pleased to respect the ceremonials, acknowledging the rival claims of God and Caesar, he offers a less exalted, less weighty, more attractive alternative to love, that saintly and severe taskmaster who calls for purity, abnegation, and undying allegiance. Instead, as this charming and clever fellow proposes, why not simply be decent, respectful, and affectionate? Is not kind man the natural prescription for mankind?

Mozart is the prince of cordiality, the prince of tolerance (who never sneers at but enjoys our foibles), the prince of kindness. His message can be distilled in different ways, but I prefer the simple injunction—listen before you talk. You might learn something which could inform your own thoughts, making them more perceptive, bearable, and winged.

♭

Beethoven is another story, closer to Haydn than to Mozart, more pinecone than hazelnut, digestible but less tender. However, no less kind than either. If Mozart's ethic of brotherhood is a day at the beach (partly sunny), where they come in all shapes and sizes, Beethoven's fraternal ideal is rather more people than person, more mankind than man, and good for all kinds of weather. Whether he was the actual or alleged author of such sentiments as Whoever loves humanity must hate humans, or I never met a human I liked as much as any tree, they are not entirely out of character. Yet no one can gainsay the ecstatic and delicate filaments of loving that fill his music. I doubt if anyone has used the notation *dolce* more frequently.

But what was he loving then? Being a rather philosophical type, well grounded in Sophocles and Shakespeare, he seemed to love loving and various other abstractions. I do not speak of his personal character and habits, which already have been psychoanalyzed to a point of ill return. (Does the identification of the Immortal Beloved really give us a clue to the interpretation of *An die ferne Geliebte*? Or are we simply relieved to know that Beethoven also was a sweaty chap with overactive glands?) Beethoven had a thing for the larger categories which embrace things. For Beethoven, the concepts of Nature, Fate (alas), and the Deity were vivid protagonists in his music drama.

♩

What happens occasionally in Haydn and Beethoven (but rarely in Mozart) is the anomalous insertion of a long passage, lasting many bars, which features exclusive reliance upon some instrumental figure drummed out incessantly and uniformly. While the harmonies and dynamics may change, motivic activity is usually primitive, sequential, or null, while the rhythmic *ostinato* and drive are unyielding and relentless. Thus, in the middle of the typical Classical symposium of ideas proposed, conversed, altered, or rejected, a strange, monolithic beast imposes, paralyzing the action and holding us by the scruff of the neck; we are charmed or terrified, depending upon the intent of this demon.

In Haydn these passages, which may be parenthetical, structurally functional, or both, are often samples of a personal glee or temper that wreaks antic (or frantic) havoc on the formal tableau. Haydn is a cunning, sure-handed burglar who robs Peter to pay Paul. Like Lola, he gets what he wants, and if he wants to tweak our nose, it is all in the day's work of a stout-hearted fellow. Haydn is Self, confident and robust. His willfulness is never conceited, but like any gifted burglar or minister, he will test the environment and exploit all the graphic bumps and gaps. Beethoven has this special pipeline to the Furies. Their harsh, unremitting wail takes hold, and as any good metaphysical journalist would do, he gives you the dreaded facts.

♀

Beethoven was so pleased with his B-flat Piano Sonata, op. 22, that at the end of the manuscript he scrawled, "This one takes the cake" (loosely translated). The development section of the first movement begins with the usual free-for-all among themes of the exposition until elements of the opening and closing themes converge into an extended passage dominated by a relentless sixteenth-note figuration. The energy of the sixteenths almost obliterates the motivic references by its sheer and faceless momentum. Harmonies and dynamics conform to rigid formulas which subjugate the musical activity to this primitive scheme. Nothing can budge the will of this implacable intensity, which finally recedes and withers into a meandering scale that settles on the dominant, announcing most demurely, or thankfully, the recapitulation. The whole passage takes up thirty-seven bars, of which only the last four are unhitched from the sixteenth-note figure. Its duration consumes nearly two-thirds of the development and one-fifth of the entire movement. The general mood of the movement, one of spirited jest and affability, is struck dumb by this tirade from on high (or down low).

Beethoven is generally considered to be the paragon of indomitable will. I rather think that it is not so much his will, but his openness that allows for such breaches of con-

duct and sense. He seems unafraid to admit all gods and
beasts, even those representing anonymous, nihilistic fury
—fury, or the neutral indifference of spontaneous creation?—into his cosmology. He tells exactly what he sees,
and some things are beyond good and evil.

ǫ

The Adagio from the Sonata, op. 22, is one of those
mystical, beatific emanations that seem to both confirm and
dispel loneliness. Such are the fruits of transport. An ele-
giac, Wordsworthian setting, where even the groves and
meadows have voices, envelops the musing, melismatic line,
as though it were the province of some wandering siren.
(In my more irreverent days, I would tell my students that
a similar Adagio in ⅜ meter, from the Piano Sonata op.
31, No. 1, but with a *grazioso* twist, suggested the portrait
of an elegant courtesan in New Orleans, who on Sunday
mornings would promenade along the main boulevard in
her best finery. Another kind of wandering siren.)

In the opus 22 Adagio, a steady eighth-note figure accompanies the main voice, mostly with repeating, three-
part, plush chords. The curious nature of these chords,
which are both dark and light, dense and buoyant, rich and
melancholy, is strangely characteristic of their naive yet all-
knowing composer. (Or, as Van Gogh said of a Beethoven
symphony, enormously complicated and simple.) In the
middle section, more urgent and chromatic versions of
these chords support the tune, but this time in a starkly
transfigured world, more a *Verklärte Nacht* of angst and terror. Then the darkness subsides, and the recapitulation and
coda restore the gentle illusions.

The uniqueness of these chords, as texture and psychology, defies description. One finds their semblance in other
composers, but rarely with the throbbing, other-worldly,

despairing quality Beethoven evokes here, and similarly in the Arioso from the Sonata, op. 110. Representing some kind of distant, choral chant, sympathetic but ominous, they condition the flights of yearning. Is it ubiquitous "dark matter," or is it merely the claims of Time whose mythic denizens unravel fate, invading the more modest, human dimensions?

ş

Matchless among the unplayables and unfathomables are the *Diabelli Variations*, op. 120, a Beethoven epic of nearly fifty minutes' duration which defies technique, memory, and, most of all, understanding. Of technical needs, Liszt put it best, declaring that Beethoven requires a little more technique than he asks for—and in this work he asks for plenty. Of memory, one had better be in grandmaster form to follow the gambits of this game, in particular the endgames of each variation, which are fabulously tricky. Of understanding, may I suggest the following scenario.

There are two essential sources of spiritual energy funding these thirty-three migratory variations based on Diabelli's innocuous waltz theme. Each of these sources is confined to motivating individual, specific variations, although a few variations are nourished by both sources. The result is a somewhat random but generally staggered sequence of two opposing characters, which delineate the fundamental geography, spiritual and structural, of the entire work.

One of these characters is clearly our old friend, indomitable Will, but, in this piece, the will of dons, ruffians, buffoons, and dictators. The other source is far less evident to our tired eyes and sated ears. A great number of these variations work best when propelled by some innocent, artless hand of nature, often streams and breezes, unselfconscious, flowing, airy, aimless; or sometimes harsher agents intervene, the rattling of boulders, molecules, gremlins. Whether stream or boulder, variations of this persuasion are remarkable for their ingenuous spontaneity.

In the end, divided justly between the grinding forces of Will and the frictionless impulses of Willlessness, the form of the whole comprises a discernible braiding of mutually attractive opposites. Needless to say, the pair becomes one in the concluding Minuet.

◊

Beethoven is the supreme architect of those territories which belong to both man and the gods. Thus there is no reason to be surprised by his interest in Sophocles and Shakespeare; he is their spiritual kin. The ultimate metaphysical drama resides in the collision between man and fate, and these three soul mates portray that battle with unerring precision and detail. Or as Schubert said of Beethoven—he composes at white heat in cold blood. For all his reputation as a turbulent, manic madman, he is yet the most objective of reporters, the most far-ranging and scientific of travelers.

What may distinguish Beethoven from Shakespeare and Sophocles, however, is a gift not unexpected for so cosmic and tolerant a chronicler. Throughout his music one always hears the voice of Man, but one also hears the voices of men and women. Such that whatever the feminine may be, there has been no scribe more faithful to its careful and caring description than Beethoven. Not simply Woman idealized, but the characters of women who nourish, who dream, who endure are present and tangible in his music. This profound tenderness—in him, in them, in his blessing and insight —is unique and offers the most priceless lesson.

Moreover, his feminism exceeded gender, and his humanity embraced all lifestyles of the living, the dead, and the nonhuman. Worship is not the proper stance, but our endless admiration will do.

ᵰ

The *Appassionata* Sonata, op. 57, is considered one of these violent melodramas which lend themselves to much heaving and anguish, affecting not only the emotions of player and listener but also the structural balances and relationships of the composition. What results frequently is a distortion of the work, reduced to the level of the player's sympathies and glands rather than that majestic tableau of countervailing forces juxtaposing the symbols of Just and Evil, the Furies and Redemption. But in handling such plots, the player must hone his conviction on the boundaries of internal logic.

The first movement is marked Allegro Assai, indicating an emphatically driving *allegro*, yet it is often played too slowly. As Edwin Fischer has pointed out, its rhythmic coin, twelve insistent eighth notes articulating the $^{12}/_8$ meter, must provide the grid from which all the rest—forms, feelings, explosions—is suspended. The momentum and current supplied by the eighth-note figure may adjust to the individual gestures of various themes and moods, but it is never turned off, and it is never less than inexorable. The explosions may be huge and outrageous, but they are signs of genuine rage or outrage, not tantrums. A noble intensity remains intact, propelled by forces more vast and more intricate than anger.

Most astonishing is that Beethoven's original sketches for this movement were strangely awkward, in fact downright clumsy and far removed from the ultimate outcome. The opening phrase ended with dreary sequences, and the expansive second theme was nowhere in sight. To realize that a mind such as Beethoven's had to stumble around before finding the convincing solution is somehow reassuring. It reminds us that a little cold-blooded self-examination can spur any of us on to those revisions necessary to unveil truth—that quality of truth which is disentangled from personal clutch and bias.

𝄞

The second movement of the opus 57 Sonata consists of a theme and variations whose tempo is marked Andante con moto. It is usually played *quasi adagio* and anything but *con moto*. The character is of a gentle march, and I am reminded that my teacher played it at the funeral ceremony of his pianist colleague Michael von Zadora. The rhythmic content of this movement proceeds from quarter notes to eighths to sixteenths to thirty-seconds, in concert with the theme and its three variations. As such there is little room for tempo modification; the unbroken arc of character and direction is explicit, supplemented by an equivalent arc of registration. For the movement unfolds steadily from bass to treble, from ground to transcendence.

In general, the tempo adjustments for theme and variation movements are predictably a function of overall structure and content. If, as in this case, the mood is unified and the elaborations throughout are overtly (arithmetically) identifiable with the theme, then the tempo will hold its course. But if the variations present contrasting reflections on the original idea, then the tempo will adjust accordingly. There is a certain academic prejudice in behalf of the former viewpoint as gospel in all circumstances, which attitude was neatly countered in an exchange with a teacher from the Juilliard School. When I queried him as to whether the tempo should remain steady in such variation movements or should change according to the different characters of each variation, he replied unhesitatingly, "The tempo should change." When I asked why, he responded with beguiling logic, "Because they are variations."

In this movement from opus 57, the tempo remains steady. For as the buffer zone between the outer movements, it is less a forum for exploring modes of consolation than a quiet prayer that ascends in step with a higher purpose, whether that be of spirit or art, humility or form.

♩

The theme of the Andante is derived from the consequent phrase of the principal theme from the first movement. The theme of the last movement of the *Appassionata* is derived from an amalgam of elements from both the antecedent and consequent phrases of the same principal theme from the first movement. Such motivic connections are sometimes quite tenuous and deceiving, but the relationships here are too patent, too strategic to dismiss. Were they consciously wrought? Was Beethoven aware of them, intending to exploit such constructs and symbols of unity? The answer is irrelevant; what he didn't know with his brain he knew with his instincts, and at this level of operation brain and instincts invariably flow to the same conclusion.

The tempo of the last movement is marked Allegro ma non troppo. Not too fast!—an injunction rarely observed, even by this correspondent; though a perpetuum mobile, it is not a headlong dash. Yes, death-defying, death-desiring, both of these in tension, held and checked; above all, resistance. Will against fate, fate the projection of will: will against will. It must be held. It must not become a tarantella of personal indulgence, a testimonial to brilliant fingers which play the main theme in the dynamic region of *forte*, instead of the *pianissimo* indicated. It is a vision of repressed as well as flung energy, more repressed than hurtling, more controlled than abandoned.

Cold-blooded Beethoven. He instructs in all matters, not least that fire is born of resolve concentrated.

𝄾

Liszt is the child of Beethoven. Transcribing and performing all the Beethoven symphonies, he demonstrates fealty to his master by all inward and outward gestures. The legacy of Beethoven—developmental techniques, dramatic freedom, structural unity—is scattered throughout the scores of Liszt. Not consistently, but in essence. The compositional posture was more public, more theatrical, permitting rhetorical excursions which would artificially steam and inflate the musical content, or would revel in epiphanies of the moment—a chord, a resolution, a silence. In some sense he was shameless, but literally that; not so much self-indulgent as without shame, without fear in acknowledging the abundant dispensations of his generous muse. And if he chose to linger on a certain harmony or phrase or figuration, it was not out of absentmindedness but by the grace of *le bon Dieu*, revealing nature and spirit in their most benevolent modes, hypnotizing us one flower or valley at a time—and then by a whole ream of flowers and valleys, iridescent and idealized.

Complementary evil was the work of Satan and Mephisto. It arrived in figures filled with mordant irony, but rigidly cold in their execution. This was the scherzo world of the nineteenth century, when jokes became demons, and demons anticipated the future machines of war. This was not funny business in Liszt, but bedeviled prophecy.

When Liszt is performed without nobility, without understanding, without respect for his forebears and his debt to them, the results are unbearable.

ọ

Child of Beethoven, Liszt was also brother to Chopin, Berlioz, and Paganini. Spiritually, Chopin made the strongest impression upon Liszt, in the sense of sanctioning and encouraging the mutual interests of music and poetry. The illuminations of poetic fantasy, whether inspired directly by literary images or indirectly by the power of intoxicating moods, became the inherently suitable script for the contents and ravishments of music.

There are pieces, such as two versions of a Berceuse in D-flat, wherein Liszt has clearly followed the Chopin model. It is useful to note the poetic and structural distinctions between Chopin's Berceuse and Liszt's second essay in this form. The lulling of Chopin's lullaby is effected by a series of progressively embellished variations superimposed upon a recurring harmonic ground, the form drifting between these two circles, one expanding and the other fixed, which mesh in consoling equilibrium. The controlling architecture of this quasi chaconne has roots which extend to Bach and before. In the Liszt Berceuse, the lulling is achieved by ecstatic surrender to chromatic harmonies equally recurrent but more addictive and restless by their pinch of anarchy. In Chopin the motion is tranquil and endlessly rotating; in Liszt the quest for timelessness and the moment of ecstasy concur in deranging the senses. Both, of course, are hauntingly beautiful. Chopin looks back, while Liszt looks ahead.

ọ

From Berlioz, whose *Symphonie fantastique* he transcribed for piano, Liszt reinforced his appetite for an inflamed and exotic rhetoric. He may have also learned something about orchestration, of which he is an underappreciated master. Apart from the occasional brassy splurges, there is often an elegant transparency of sound—a counterpoint of timbres

—in Liszt's orchestration, which, as evident from his other creative gifts, is prophetic of twentieth-century developments.

The Paganini influence was pertinent but tangential, for Liszt already possessed a diabolical technique and was not immune to the rewards of cultivating his public persona. More functional was the transformation of certain violin gestures and sonorities into the appropriate piano style. One such piece which strikingly exploits this transfer is the *Transcendental* Etude no. 2 in A Minor.

In this piece one encounters pianistic versions of *pizzicati*, double stops, and bow technique. But one also hears something else, and far more important. One hears a succinct rhythmic motive, four repeated notes of the same pitch, elaborated in extraordinarily fertile and pungent ways, occupying 102 bars as the sole weapon of the compositional arsenal. In a style absolutely beholden to Beethoven, a single neutral and multipurpose idea is brandished through multiple, panoramic stratagems, establishing total authority and integrity over the form. Such an intricate, responsible command of the compositional process can occur only in the minds and operations of very great composers. The piece is also vivid and exciting, but that its total content is entirely propagated from the material of this fixed core is confirming sign of structural genius.

♭

The Liszt B Minor Piano Sonata is considered the very prototype of thematic transformation. For good reason, since every aspect of its substantial length derives from a limited set of generating motives. The (relatively) Spartan materials are disseminated through a vast network of shapes and shadows, their guises both conspicuous and unobtrusive. Inverse in expressive sequence to the transformation

Liszt devises for his A Major Piano Concerto, a pounding, heathen bass motive near the beginning of the B Minor Sonata is later unveiled as the origin of the lyrical second theme, now tender and devotional. Less obvious but no less interesting is the genesis for the bass line accompanying this theme, a vestigial, but functional, reprise of the work's introductory motive, the rising seventh and stepwise descent in bars 2 and 3. On the whole, the musical fabric is not as taut or monotheistic as the Schoenberg practice of extracting all materials from the same row of intervals, but it anticipates this method by its special chemistry of intellectual rigor and dramatic fantasy.

The ways of performing this piece rather sharply divide into two opposite camps. One usually hears the individual themes and ideas typecast in all their singular, expressive fervor, but neglectful of motivic and structural relationships. Less favored and more refined is that interpretation which conditions the thematic variables according to their primary sources and to their role in the architecture. Ideal would be a synthesizing vision which could make many out of one and one out of many.

♭

Twenty years before Wagner composed *Tristan und Isolde*, the work which was both emblem and catalyst to the then imminent breakdown of tonality, Liszt was writing harmonic progressions which moved, sounded, and quacked like those-to-be of his future son-in-law. Wagner's debt to Liszt was directly confirmed in a letter to Hans von Bülow (another son-in-law of Liszt's by the same enterprising daughter): "There are many matters on which we are quite frank among ourselves (for instance, that since my acquaintance with Liszt's compositions my treatment of harmony has become very different from what it was for-

merly), but it is indiscreet, to say the least, of friend Pohl
to babble this secret to the entire world."

In this continuous vein of harmonic experimentation and
discovery, the later works of Liszt are replete with uncanny
omens and agents of tonal dissolution. A strange, evanes-
cent fragrance overtakes these compositions, for the elements of harmonic instability—the augmented chords, the
tritones, the sevenths, the unresolved dissonances—are frequently harbored in a kind of surreptitious stasis, limblessly
floating, unmoored as though on a ship of the damned. A
piece such as *Nuages gris* can be heard in one of two ways:
as token of that limbo which precedes and succeeds all
cataclysms, token then of this century; or, less likely and
more inspiring, as sample of that neutral chaos which is
our birthright and environment, more uncertain than chaotic, more free than fated. Of course, if you insist that the
piece is really and only about "grey clouds," I will tem-
porarily concede the point—until you come to your senses,
all six of them.

ǫ

Liszt was perhaps the most generous of the great musicians. He consistently advocated and performed the works
of other composers while at the same time nurturing a class
of extraordinary piano students to whom he never charged
a fee. One tends to scorn him for apparently casual excesses,
such as his transcriptions of the scores of third-rate composers, when in fact it was but his intention to further their
careers by publicizing their music. It is true, as Debussy
wrote, that "sometimes he gets on easy terms with [music]
and frankly takes it on his knee." But it is also the case,
as Debussy acknowledged in the same article, that "the
undeniable beauty of Liszt's work arises, I believe, from the
fact that his love for music excluded every other kind of
emotion."

It is the conventional wisdom that both the compositions and persona of Liszt tend to magnify private feelings to the level of public and theatrical display. I would suggest that an alternative view is plausible, in that Liszt discovered an extremely personal and poetic language for representing the grand and universal themes: illusion, fantasy, devotion, and evil. He was, in particular, a poet of love and of nothingness, of that love which is indiscriminate only in its charitable benevolence, of that void which both evokes and disintegrates barbarism.

ọ

In our playing, as we maneuver through both the nourishing veils of doubt and the "incomparable vivacity of life," we need navigational tools, compass and sail, to move from here to there. The welter of forms and the gnawing of uncertainty can inhibit and deflect us, can make us stumble in the labyrinth, or worse, make us race by ignorantly. We need some mechanism of balance and steering to effect flexible passage through the piece. It must be sufficiently free to describe all the lovely sights along the way and sufficiently steady to stay afloat and on course.

The answer should lie in some process which uses time efficiently. But which time? The time that regulates, or the time that liberates? I would suggest a qualification of Mozart's valid dictum: right hand *rubato*, left hand in strict time. There is a simple (but not so simple) formula which can accommodate both instincts, steadiness and freedom, and which is intrinsic to the very notation and scansion of time.

Divide the rhythmic material into its basic constituents, strong beats and weak beats. The function of the strong beats is to secure and stabilize the musical flow by acting as marshal and marker of the basic tempo. As such they occur at wholly predictable time intervals, giving to them

a magisterial presence and authority. The weak beats, however, are more the preserve of exploratory gestures, often
less grave and more probing. They can be lighter, more
light-hearted, more playful; or they can be more brutal and
demanding, or more lyrical and expansive.

The colloquy between these two agents of diction and
flow, the one more stable (but not imposing, rather serene),
and the other more free, can create a metabolism of "perpetual" motion which carries the piece along and provides
a stately, expansive bearing. It qualifies, but does not at all
disqualify, Mozart's rule.

𝄇

The relationship of melody to accompaniment—as a
matter of characterization, dynamics, and timing—is a subject that will not go away. Measurement of these two independent but corresponding orbits cries out for ever-new
refinements and insights to plot their different curves; how
do they match and how do they differ, as though forming
an experienced ballroom couple who work in perfect but
perilous alliance, trapped in a shared destiny of unshared
origins.

Somewhere it was reported that the conductor Klaus
Tennstedt said it was more important to conduct the second violins than the first, therefore more crucial to define
the accompaniment than the melody, the ground than the
figure. And then I remember my teacher mentioning that
the composer and conductor Alexander von Zemlinsky
(who was the teacher of Schoenberg) observed that the first
and second violins should never play in the same tempo.

But before pleading for the permanent separation of melodic interests from background voices, one must temper
that plea by remembering the common purpose and intimate communion of these two dimensions, however different their functions and dispositions. After all, they should

talk to each other occasionally, reinforce and support the expressive goals, and harmonize their interests, though their embrace be back-to-back. For by the incidents and accidents of their exchange, new chemistries of sound and character emerge, while the essential paradox of the one and the many is perpetually confronted. Nevertheless, the odes and elegies of the soloist will always stir images of loneliness, deliverance, or odyssey, never fully abated by the more or less friendly companions of the accompanying voices.

℘

Soirée dans Grenade from the suite *Estampes* by Debussy, is a habanera to be played, according to the composer's instructions, with "nonchalant grace." In bar 17, marked *tempo giusto*, my excellent student neglects to articulate the chords with sufficient *brio* to sustain the *élan* of the piece, its special recipe of bittersweet irony and dark omen. Probing about, I suggest, "Like the sounds of pre-Castro Cuba." That gets nowhere. "Like the brass section of the big bands, Tommy Dorsey or Harry James." Some improvement now. But then we must return to the opening motive, where the dotted rhythm comes out slack, without the "nonchalant grace," without the characteristic indifference to indifferent fate. A quick stab: "the sixteenth note like the false kiss of the seducer." Ah, that's better; and so we roll the dice and unravel the meaning, stepping gingerly on hot coals until the accidents mold into purpose.

In one of his lectures, the composer Anton Webern speaks rather disparagingly of the listening habits of the masses, saying that they are not content unless they can imagine a green field or a blue sky or something of that nature. From a great composer who above all sought precision and clarity, who devoutly believed in the self-referential capacity of musical ideas to communicate through their content and elaboration alone, I must acknowledge that I find this view incompatible with my own affinity for metaphor and characterization. I have no answer except to say, why not? Why not a green field or a blue sky? Why not the appropriate image or attribute? The purpose is but to intensify, to illuminate, to heighten the charge and cathexis of those same musical ideas, their shapes and elaborations. There is, of course, always the danger of getting it wrong. But I would suggest that cultivating this danger is the best way of getting it right, either as thing-in-itself or as sample of that expressive territory which music must always seek out.

ò

My teacher always asked, What is the character of the piece? Now we all know that finding the right character is as shady and elusive a business as finding the criminal in a Sherlock Holmes mystery. There are many false leads before the true identity is established, yet pursuing those leads heightens the surprise of revelation. When Josef Hofmann began a piece too casually at his lesson, his formidable teacher, Anton Rubinstein, stopped him abruptly to ask the very same question: "What is the character of the piece? Is it dramatic, tragic, lyric, romantic, humorous, heroic, sublime, mystic—what?"

It must be something. Itself? But that is a barren tautology, self-satisfied as well as self-sufficient. Certainly the internal structure of a composition is documentary evidence of its validity. But even structure, in music or chess or physics, has its moods, shadings, quirks, and charms. And what does this structure support? Is it a giant erector set? Or is it an edifice with parapets, dungeons, balconies, steeples, and chambers, concealing both false and propitious corridors?

Unique specimens also have their common properties, as incomparable beings are yet comparable. What is different, what is the same—that is the work of scientists, artists, poets. If one proceeds on the assumption that every musician, as every soul, has some poetry within, then one cannot ignore what the poet sees and differentiates by his faithful study. That we use words to describe musical character is but a convenience. That the character be identified is an obligation.

I hope that the young people will flourish, will gradually leave their wired bedrooms, will study what is eternally abundant and delightful in the species and vegetation around them, and that they will take part in a new music as supple as the wind, as complex as the anatomy of a leaf, and as beguiling as the colors of tropical birds and the forests to be replenished. The burgeoning political movements in behalf of both human rights and the environment—and their charge to musicians to act as spokespeople for the chained, the inarticulate, and the natural world—are deeply encouraging.

Playing the piano is a private task of universal possibilities. As others have said, if we all played the piano it would be a much happier world. What is most compelling about the piano, finally, is its enduring fascination. There is no limit to its intrigue and study. And with luck and dedication we not only improve but come closer to the stories of transcendence and discovery.

To be human is to explore. In this quest the piano can be an ideal companion and source, a kind of metaphorical telescope which can read both the properties of stars and the markings of distant wildflowers. By grace of this clutter of wires, felts, and hammers, the mysteries of solitude and communion are open to all.

CODA

The left hand (as accompaniment) serves as steward, but-
ler, valet, duenna, nursemaid, and perfect gentleman. It is
also captain of the ship, referee, and philanthropist. The
right hand (as melody) is quixotic, temperamental, manic-
depressive, demanding, and angel of mercy. The two coexist, sometimes peacefully.

♩

The argument goes round and round. Leon Botstein, the
professional musician who doubles as president of Bard Col-

lege, declares that the sciences should be preeminent in the education of our young. For George Bernard Shaw, amateur musician, the humanities come first. Both are right. Music and mathematics are contrasting expressions of the same laws. But since mathematics, of the two, is the more capricious, one should start with music, province of the great truths that prepare for life and death.

ꝰ

Melodies composed for the piano have their distinct colors and touches, yet they possess characteristics of sound appropriate to all other existing and conceivable instruments. To spin out beautiful tunes on the piano, one has to know bowing, flutter-tonguing, the pungent groans of the kayagum, and the shudderings and sighings of the oud.

ꝰ

"Architecture is frozen music," so Goethe instructs. Then music must be fluid (boiling?) architecture. Form in flux: Fred Astaire.

ꝰ

Terence: "Nothing human is alien to me." Schumann was daft much of the time. Music is daft through and through. The most innocent tune of Mozart would never survive without fever blisters attached, without being haunted by the ghosts of Dido, or of Orpheus, the careless slayer of his beloved.

ꝰ

One must play the right notes at the right time. But if forced to choose between the right notes absent of character or some wrong notes for the right cause, the choice is clear. Certain great artists can never play perfectly. Perfection is too mundane, brittle, uptight for those who make music the way God makes trees.

ꝰ

Music is an illusion designed to embellish and deceive coarse reality. But deprived of music, dry reality becomes an illusory moment perpetually fading, without content or contentment. Fortunately, wind and water oblige when the voice is stilled; therefore music is everywhere, and reality exists (tenuously).

♩

Should the student polish up a few pieces over and over again, refining touch and sensibility? Or should the student learn to deal, however conditionally, with many different pieces, augmenting repertoire, experience, and means of judgment? Quality vs. quantity, a tedious argument to be resolved in favor of productivity: i.e., a goodly amount well done, some chiseled and some not.

♩

If one wants to know how to read nature and how to read music, consult the notebooks of Gerard Manley Hopkins, and, in particular, his observations and epiphanies describing the motion of waves. For a further elucidation, read the article by the poet Ben Belitt, from the magazine *Salmagundi* (Spring-Summer 1993). From such testimony we discover how the world and water may illuminate us, may "tickle" us (as in the inscription to Ravel's *Jeux d'eau*), until we are purged, ready to see and hear.

♩

In the age of television, epitome and model for all forms of communication, the essential gift for success is imperturbability: immunity to pressure and the sweaty demons of inspiration. Therefore, by today's standards, cruising confidently through the music may be prized more than examining those urgent declamations and rhetorical quandaries which issue from having conversations with the gods.

♩

Claudio Arrau on Liszt: "Declamation. Uninhibited expression. One must not feel ashamed of playing this music. The idea that he can be 'corrected' by understatement is utterly wrong."

Continuing: "In general, when actors in this country do Shakespeare, they almost always underplay. They act as if they are ashamed of their roles and lives. They think people will laugh at them. If they would go all out, all the way, they would find that people would not laugh but be riveted. They would weep. Certain performances must make you weep, either for the sheer beauty of it or for the depth of feeling." [From *The Essential Piano Quarterly*]

♭

The kids in our elementary schools may be spiritually further advanced than their colleagues who attend high school. Concern for health, for animals, for the environment, as well as a certain sobriety in the face of commercial pandering and enticement, is more evident among preteens than among some of the jaded adolescents whose souls have already begun to fade. While the older students are too frequently victims of economic angst and cynicism, younger children seem to be benefiting from the holistic and civilizing messages of dedicated teachers and parents.

♭

Many thoughtful observers point out that the decline in academic standards is concurrent with and consequent to the expansion of the educational franchise, a function of the number of people necessarily herded into the system. No doubt. But the decline in the status of the teacher is equally relevant. Creative people may well starve; that is a random by-product of their genius and independence. But teachers, who explain and celebrate creation, must be afforded the privileges and dignity of statesmen, for they carry the welfare of the state—and of civilization—on their back.

◊

The problem with society is the very nature of available jobs. (Consult the works of the anthropologist Edward Sapir.) For if humans made things instead of being things in their making and selling, dispositions would be sunnier, eggs would be good for you, and people would have a center instead of parts. Which amounts to the oft-stated difference between work and labor.

◊

In the days of Cole Porter and Hoagy Carmichael, Gary Cooper and Bette Davis, the popular culture flowed smoothly into and around the serious culture. Rather suddenly that continuum has been broken. Much of the current cinematic and musical fare seems to revel in mantras of bluster and nihilism that would destabilize, mock, and overwhelm the powers of discrimination. From this rather monolithic perspective, the serious culture is regarded as but a lame anachronism.

The tension, indeed the schism, between these two worldviews has sharpened dramatically. Given this frame, and given the conviction that one of these views may be dangerously exaggerated, should one sit idly by, smile indulgently, and passively acquiesce—kids playing?

Meanwhile, on aesthetic and psychological grounds, let us not forget that a work of art endures to the degree that the response it elicits is *both* direct and considered, *both* emotional and thoughtful.

◊

Question: Can the electronic culture be salvaged? Can a worldview so amorphous, preliterate, and transient be adapted to civilized standards? Can thought withstand impulse when the chimera of total and instant availability is let loose?

The turning point will come quickly. Somebody will

point out, convincingly, that reality can only be comprehended, not apprehended, and that therefore Virtual Reality is a fake. Soon after, people will throw away their
television sets and begin to make things and grow things
with their hands. And then some latter-day successor to
Goethe will establish, conclusively, that human reality cannot be satisfied unless body, soul, mind, and spirit work
together, and in a manner which is coherently conceived,
felt, and executed.

$\natural$

When all is said and done, the melody is still the queen
bee. All the other voices must serve the colony by diligently
supporting her. For without her health, well-being, and
radiance, the colony—and the piece—will not survive.

$\natural$

The critical goal, the be-all and end-all, the unbearable
lightness at the end of the rainbow, is the quality of *cantabile*. But *cantabile* without *parlando* is like a song without
words. And every song has words, especially those wordless
words which resonate the full sentiment without any betrayal by pale, ambiguous language. For it is not words
which constitute *parlando* but rather their roots and branchings, their souls and grammar. In a word, they call it
eloquence.

$\natural$

A useful formula for many blushing themes and unbridled chants: the melody *parlando*, the accompaniment
cantabile. For *cantabile*, as the language of binding sentiments and textures, is often the desired inflection of the
supporting voices. The melody, more garrulous of its griefs
and more brazen in its vows and protests, can well adopt a
parlando touch to articulate its several claims. That is, when
the occasion demands.

$\natural$

Melodies speak in the voices of lovers, warriors, and priests. Such is the expectation. But consider also the memory, the history, the wisdom and suffering contained within certain melodies. By the standard of that debt, such tones must echo the voices of generations ago. So that those with the keenest memories of their grandparents may well have the best shot at reproducing the tender tribulations of the melodic content, its dream and weariness, its weave and questions.

♭

Brahms said that the bass line was of equal importance to the soprano. Together they are the twin suspensions, poles, and boundaries of the musical material. To be intelligible, the sound must be framed. The viscous content within must not overflow. It may erupt, explode, devastate, but not compromise the stability, sanctity, and order of this universe. Otherwise the music, in its perspective and illusion of permanence, will crumple like a milk carton.

♭

To say a kind (if reluctant) word about rock and roll, in its tone and lyrics the thread of empowerment runs through. People of all races and graces are summoned to the starting line in the name of equal opportunity. But the message has been badly bungled, degenerating into trite solipsisms of me-first lust and vengeance. The self-indulgent shaker and breaker becomes a rebel without a cause.

♭

What one looks for in a student: chaos and discipline: that is, the feeling for abandon, the knack for stray, incongruous, and inspired intuitions—matched by the hard-boiled work ethic of a surveyor, a blacksmith, a cardsharp.

♭

What a student needs in a teacher: balance. Not so much of the temperance type (on the one hand, on the other hand); but projecting a model of personality which reflects every aspect of human nature, emphasizing the good, and then balancing all the parts.

𝄞

The least developed faculty among our youth? Again I reiterate, the gift for irony. Its absence partly derives from a modern culture horribly distorted by contentious media and politicians who constantly and hypocritically accuse: "You can't have it both ways!" Thus they beat each other over the head, while the supreme tactic for estimating life and art vanishes. For "both" is the only civilized response to competing claims and ideologies. Perhaps not both equally, but both viewpoints, even though incongruous, acknowledged to some tangible degree. And handled with ease and wry humor.

Absent irony, cynicism and greed take over.

𝄞

The psychological redemption of pianists, children, and other interested parties may evolve from stage to stage along the following lines: beginning with given rage, the mother of all feelings, transformed by will and encouragement into a sense of outrage; progressing to an awareness of injustice, and subsequently generalizing toward empathy and a concept of justice; then leading to a spirit of conviction, affirmation, and, finally, joy. Thus hatred and self-hatred, the sentries of fear, may mollify toward kindness, and musicians may spread the gospel.

But rage can never be fully vanquished, only sublimated—a process of moderation and fulfillment which should be an underlying message of all education. For rage, acknowledged and ameliorated, may well be a fundamental source of fantasy and creativity.

𝄞

The Hungarian side of Brahms, the Turkish side of Mozart, or Chopin as both Polish and French, Stravinsky as French and Russian: these are the obvious examples of a psychological truth easily buried under the monolithic habits of Style and its paid courier, Reason. For every thought, melody, and creation also contain their contrary characters, without which there remain only tired platitudes. Of all the composers, Mozart is most prone to the Arabian Nights and the absurdists, Beethoven to the Marx Brothers, Haydn to Beckett and Buster Keaton, Wagner to Fantasy Island.

♩

The nature of light: particles or waves? The nature of melodic lines: particles or waves? Of course, both models, each indispensable. Not alternating, but both simultaneously.

♩

Of the nine Muses, three of them are assigned to music. These are Euterpe, Erato, and Polyhymnia, guardians, respectively, of the flute, the lyre, and sacred song. Thus the origins of music, from meadow to courtyard to temple, or thereabouts. But can one overlook comedy, poetry, tragedy, above all Terpsichore, the Muse of dance, when we study and make music? And as for history and astronomy, are there not also ample references in our scores?

♩

The fingertip is a bee that extracts nectar from the note. The fingertip is a moth targeted by the note's inviting flames. The fingertip is a caterpillar crawling through the shoals and sinews of each key.

♩

The percentage of the number of finalists or semifinalists in competitions who actually study with members of the jury is often outrageous. Even more absurd is the practice of ranking students by some artificial amount of points

earned, as though musical qualities could be itemized and to-
taled. Defenders of this method suggest that it is designed to
negate the prior problem, overt partisanship. It doesn't.

ꝙ

Throughout these pages I have insufficiently distinguished between a general concept of "relaxation" and
certain of its deceptive homilies, to the unfair detriment of
the former. For the simple grandeur which is implicit in
both the text and presentation of classical music requires
an attitude of ease and communion with the sources of
inspiration. Those injunctions which tell us not to rush,
not to crush the musical thoughts are essential and obligatory. These principles, and others more pragmatic, call
forth an expansiveness of soul which rests upon a controlled,
rounded breathing informing the entire apparatus of muscular and mental forces. More equilibrium than relaxation
as such, but an attitude most cordial to its message.

ꝙ

As appropriate, a discreet dose of pedal provided directly
after the melody tone is struck will yield a kind of "halo"
effect for sustaining the *legato*. Busoni mentions this.
Though not easy to coordinate, it nevertheless should be
included in the arsenal of cosmetic and cosmic tricks.

ꝙ

Legato is the conundrum and cross that pianists have to
bear. Automatically we think: connect. Yet simple physical
connection is but one—often mechanical—tool. *Legato* is a
state of mind. It is like crossing the Rubicon or the Red
Sea without pontoons. It is more a matter of gesture, dynamics, and timing, but understanding the structure of the
phrase is the critical premise.

ꝙ

Bill Cosby laments that aging men grow hair in every
conceivable and useless place except where they most want

it—on top of their heads. Similarly, our grand pianos produce bright or sonorous tone in every conceivable register except where we really *need* it—in the treble.

And then, to compound the liability, our weakest fingers are responsible for the most crucial notes!

ọ

I return to the thumb of the left hand in its role as center of the sound, as granary and ballast for the twitterings and rumblings that surround it. I have always thought of this thumb as the French horn of the piano orchestra. But too many bobbles and croakings for my weary ears have caused me to modify this image. And so now I think of it as surrogate for the cello, more ministering to than minister of the sound. Now I tell my students—don't blow, rather bow. Until they start muddling it up.

A sign of aging.

ọ

As a precise, neat, and cryptic model of motivic elaboration, the development section of Beethoven's first piano sonata, op. 2, no. 1, is both apt and exemplary. Perhaps nothing is more important for the student than the awareness of evolving phrase structures, their inner workings and metamorphoses. For many students (people) are psychologically and operationally static. It is on or off, fast or slow, loud or soft, A or B, one or the other. But the destinies of effectively articulated phrases refute this lumbering polarity. The many twists and turns, contrasts and contradictions, accidents and obstacles reflect the very stuff of life and the vault of music. It comes down to a kind of freedom then, but of that kind which knows the orbits of the planets.

ọ

The student says, "I am uncomfortable playing it this way." But that is our job as teachers, to confront and to challenge the student. Not to teach what is natural for them, but what is unnatural, what they don't know, or, more likely, what is buried within. The whole package of vital statistics, apposite images, and mystical insights must be put on the table. Eventually the students will mix and match, pick and choose. But for now it is either all or that nothing which is but a frozen fraction of the all, our own lazy habits compounding theirs.

֍

No grammar, no drama.

֍

The two words (or concepts) one rarely finds in musical criticism: creative and imaginative. Is this a deficiency of the composer/performer or of the reviewer? Or is it simply another chapter in the sordid career of deconstructionism, the latest and most baroque version of that ancient chronicle, the critic's revenge.

֍

Two, three, four, five, and more players all expressing the same feelings with the same voice, each detail and nuance uniformly articulated. Thus the prevailing chamber-music ideal, appealing to the lowest common denominator of aesthetic taste. But why write chamber music if the musical content and personality should never vary? And what happened to the symposium ideal, several individual voices engaged in passionate exchange on common topics?

This current shrinkage may be attributed to the BMW syndrome, in which smoothness and efficiency become the ultimate standard uniting both critic and consumer in perfect lockstep. For any deviation from this musical norm can be easily identified, precluding the need (or gift) for imaginative survey of those disparate voices essential to enlightened discussion, to chamber music.

֍

The appropriate curriculum for a music student, other than the relevant and essential topics of music theory and

music history, should comprise: deductive reasoning, mythology, ecology, allied arts and literature, languages, cosmology, chivalry, and the tango.

♀

The composer composes the notes, the performer composes the sounds. Both are indispensable, but only one
can survive without the other. Nevertheless, indestructible
notes are but the prelude to transient and consoling sounds.

♀

Humor is for the gods, ruthless in their games and
mockeries. Whimsy is for music, without tiffs, envies, or
butts. Music is a science for survival in the face of uncertain
times and cosmic indifference. When Beethoven laughs, he
does not ridicule or humiliate. Rather he draws a picture
of inconstancy as a lesson for deriving grace, footwork, wisdom. The uncertainty principle is met by a smile and a
wink, gallantry to match life's banana peel. Charlie Chap-
lin. See the last movement of Beethoven's piano sonata, op.
10, no. 3.

♀

If, according to Shelley, a poem is but an inadequate
transposition of the original creative vision, and if, according to Busoni, a musical performance is but a conditional
transposition of an original score already transposed and
once-removed, then what hope can we entertain of a so-
called "objective" performance, as though reconstituting a
score damaged at birth and/or stillborn?

Not to mention a few other insurmountable variables,
such as changing halls, acoustics, instruments, biorhythms,
conceptions, and cultural contexts. Besides, any score that
has survived the exigencies of history can only be touched,
never possessed. Otherwise innocent (guiltless) computers
could create, and could understand the mystery of creation.
And composers would always hear their music played the

same way, without risk or danger or adventure. Then music
would belong to the museums.

̬

Like Gaul, the musical map of meanings is divided into
three parts: (1) formal information, confined to purely musical parameters of pitch, duration, dynamics, etc., in their
various and intricate relationships; (2) the spectrum of psychological moods, generalized zones of feeling attached to
the different modes and their guises as conditioned by time
and habit; (3) the specific yet elusive poetic imagery produced by various combinations and patterns of sound, a
veritable carnival of metaphorical associations which unfolding music projects as a cinema of the soul and spirit,
Prometheus unbound. But a private cinema, which even
the greatest skill and conviction can never entirely convey.

These three tracks live in a ménage à trois, forever mutually dependent yet forever jealous of their own authority.

̬

An informed interpretation of a musical composition
should consider two contrary yet complementary perspectives: an idealized Platonic vision of the work that presumes
a stable, inviolable conception; an Aristotelian inquiry that
engages and sorts out the work's empirical details and
events. Therefore: solemnly guard the temple against un-
welcome intruders; but respond gladly and conscientiously
to the refinements of its carvings and architectural features.

Lurking in the background are the feudal bosses classical
and romantic, corresponding roughly to form and fantasy.
However, these Mafiosi have been almost fatally wounded
by sustained verbal abuse. In fact, they have become havens
of misconception, in particular with respect to the unity/
variety syndrome. For the concept of classical, although
conventionally a symbol of unadorned form, in reality stands
for a process of multiple themes, details, articulations in

dialectical balance, especially as it applies to music of the Classical era. Romantic music, on the other hand, is signified by a single-minded arc of unwavering flight using simpler structures, basic forms, and fewer contrasting ideas, despite the romantic reputation for fantastic designs and detours.

Perhaps we need the old Greeks to come to the rescue once again.

ọ

When people (not least musicians) think of musical unity, they think of one idea, one tempo, one affect, one direction, one destiny. When composers (more rarely, performers) think of musical unity, they assimilate this one-sided monomania into a much broader picture. Artists, fierce partisans of nature, portray unity as a compound of complementary images and ideas. The difference is between a great cathedral and a functional skyscraper. In musical terms, contrasting motives, rhythms, and designs, bound by compatible threads, coexist within a landscape of variables at once diverse and symbiotic. Repetition is the starting point, but its progeny are willfully abundant, bordering on the antic and rebellious. In the name of life, in the name of fun, in the name of accurate reporting.

A genuine performance balances the variables, however contradictory, in supple if complex equilibrium. The result is not a fifty-fifty compromise between unity and variety but a mutual soaking of their full values. For the unity achieved by the reconciliation of opposites is more profound than the unity derived from a blinkered momentum.

ọ

The charm of music resides in its indiscriminate appeal to all the senses. A performance which has taste, vision, and a beautiful sound fashioned by the appropriate touch will be savored by the discriminating audience.

ọ

There exist only the mass media and the mediated mass. They have become exactly the same thing—a perfect congruence reflecting the values of envy and indulgence so endemic to contemporary society. That charitable instincts can yet survive is testimony to the amazing resources of human genes and ingenuity.

◊

In the space of a piano octave there are seven white keys and five black keys. Since the white keys are more plentiful and more distant from both hand and eye, they are comparatively harder to differentiate—and to play (in particular, the bufferless zones of E-natural/F-natural and B-natural/C-natural). The black keys are like icebergs which jut out from the foamy sea of white keys. Perching on them is much less of a problem. Moral: for balance, execution, and evenness, concentrate a little more on the white keys.

◊

My insistence on the separation of powers and speech patterns between the hands may lead inadvertently to a confining image of the left-hand role in homophonic textures. The multiple duties of the accompaniment—metric, harmonic, and as general support system—should not negate its contrapuntal implications. There is an enormous vitality latent in the various patterns of skillfully written accompaniments. Their muse, while not as volatile or wanton as the melody's source, requires an internal dynamic and articulation no less sensitive. However formal or fated the background elements, the laws of biology and rhetoric still operate there. Nothing is immune from spontaneous or sympathetic combustion.

◊

How baffling and astonishing when the pop technocrats refer to our instrument as an "acoustical piano," as though it were a strange subspecies distinct from relevant and contemporary keyboards. Besides, "the piano recital is dead," goes the refrain of many experienced commentators. Phooey! Maybe it's the establishment which is dead, but when a great chunk of Western and other histories is available to be expressed in noblest form through one instrument by one person in a meeting most intimate and grand, then the funeral is premature. On the contrary, I anticipate a rebirth combining the wisdoms of several generations, forming the basis of a piano playing more personal, more direct, more free, more powerful, more precisely articulated. Hold on to your hats. Wait until you hear the next crop of young artists.

ọ̇

The chortling of bassoons: a good model for certain left-hand motoric accompaniments and passagework.

ọ̇

Nevertheless, when I asked Gunther Schuller about a particular left-hand passage from a piano piece he composed for me—"Do you want this to sound like a bassoon or a horn?" —he replied, "No, like a piano." An apt and useful lesson.

ọ̇

Speaking of lessons, listen to Schnabel's recordings of the Beethoven piano sonatas. The capacity for digesting and executing the information derived from the score is exemplary, multifaceted, and profound. Is it objective? Far more than the pseudo-objectivity of today's piano monarchs, which is often but a courteous acquiescence that rounds off and squares up the volatile brushwork of Beethoven. Those details, often minute, which are most remarkable and evocative in the score become easily domesticated to the interests of loving generalities and filial respect. But respect is not fidelity.

ọ̇

When Ferdinand Ries, a favorite piano student of Beethoven's, played a wrong note in the Variations, op. 34, composed by his teacher, the Master was indulgent, referring to the slip as a mere accident. But when Ries played the passage in question with the wrong *character*, the Master became visibly angry, such that the student had to repeat the passage seventeen times in order to satisfy his teacher.

Ries claimed that he played the passage just as well as Beethoven did, an assertion, which, if correct, might alarm some of us in the teaching fraternity who are less gifted than Beethoven. Namely, do the students really see through our protests and pretensions?

♀

When one plays Beethoven one must serve Beethoven. No, one must represent Beethoven. No, one must be Beethoven.

♀

The main problem: balancing variety with unity, events with momentum, inflections with structure. By current standards, events are often bleached or submerged, many times in favor of a prevalent "long line" which intends to curry favor without, however, favoring the individual and idiomatic curries.

♀

I am always struck by the model and standard of the neighborhood piano teacher. Their devotion, curiosity, and loyalty to both child and cause inspire us far more than the examples of our presidents, CEO's, and other pros. One is grateful for their indomitable spirit in the face of merciless odds. And they prove that music and piano playing are ultimate, sustaining gifts.

♀

Eloquence and grace, vitality and charm, faithfulness and vision: the game of life, the life of music.